TWENTIETH CENTURY
INTERPRETATIONS

MAYNARD MACK, *Series Editor*
Yale University

NOW AVAILABLE
Collections of Critical Essays
ON

TWENTIETH CENTURY INTERPRETATIONS
OF

THE PORTRAIT
OF A LADY

A Collection of Critical Essays

Edited by

PETER BUITENHUIS

Prentice-Hall, Inc. A SPECTRUM BOOK *Englewood Cliffs, N. J.*

Contents

Introduction

by Peter Buitenhuis

One sure sign of a distinguished work of art is in the number and variety of interpretations that have been made of it. *The Portrait of a Lady* has provoked scores of scholars and critics into commentary and counter commentary, particularly in the last fifteen years. The task of selecting essays for this volume has been correspondingly difficult and, in the last analysis, arbitrary. What I have sought most to represent is the range of opinion about the meaning and value of this celebrated novel. This has meant that I have had to slight some excellent studies on the novel's sources, influences, and textual problems.

It should be no surprise to discover that *The Portrait of a Lady* was not always so celebrated. Like any major work of art, it explored new territory and succeeded in confusing and putting off many of its early readers. Henry Adams, the novelist and historian, a good friend of Henry James, admitted that he "broke down on *The Portrait of a Lady*," although, he added, "some of my friends, of whose judgment I think highly, admire it warmly, and find it deeply interesting." [1] His wife was not so diplomatic. She wrote of the novel: "It's not that he 'bites off more than he can chaw' . . . but he chaws more than he bites off." [2] In England, on first publication, the novel had a chilly reception for the most part. Reviewers objected to James's aestheticism and to his book's length. Several critics complained that it was left unfinished. Part of the resentment against the novel probably stemmed from Isabel Archer's temerity in rejecting the proposal of an English lord, a subject on which English critics had shown a considerable touchiness in earlier reviews of James's work.[3] In the United States *The Portrait* received a better press. For some reason, American reviewers reacted more favorably to its analytical method and to its characterization, particularly of Isabel. Two influential critics con-

[1] *The Letters of Henry Adams*, ed. W. C. Ford (Boston, 1930), I, 333.
[2] *Letters of Mrs. Henry Adams*, ed. Ward Thoron (Boston, 1936), 306.
[3] James refers ironically to critical treatment of his own story "An International Episode" (1879) in his essay "The Art of Fiction." He quotes a critic who took exception to "Bostonian nymphs" [who] "rejected English dukes for psychological reasons." See *The Future of the Novel*, ed. Leon Edel (New York, 1956), 22.

sidered that *The Portrait of a Lady* came near to perfection as a novel of character development.[4]

As a consequence, when Henry James came back to visit the United States in the winter of 1881, after an absence of six years, he was agreeably surprised to find himself lionized. In Europe, he pointed out to a friend, he was ignored.[5] James was exaggerating, for by this time he had become a welcome guest at many London dinner tables; his work had found an equal welcome from many periodicals there. No doubt, however, in America James felt himself to be a bigger frog in a smaller literary puddle, and was not above the vanity of enjoying his fame.

Henry James was born in New York in 1843, but he spent much of his childhood abroad. His father, Henry, Sr., had been left a large fortune and took his wife and children on extensive travels through Europe. Henry and his elder brother, William, later to become the famous philosopher, were consequently subjected to a cosmopolitan but somewhat sporadic education. Henry, smaller and less active than his brilliant brother, frequently felt outclassed by him. While William was out at play with the bigger boys, Henry stayed behind at home finding his experience with his nose in the novels of Dickens, Thackeray, Trollope, and other popular but now less known Victorians. When out, he often mooned about by himself, playing the role of spectator. It was one he was admirably equipped to take and it became his characteristic stance as a novelist. As a child, he used to gaze through the railings at the livestock on an estate that then remained at the northeast corner of Eighteenth Street and Broadway in New York. "There," he wrote in his autobiography, "was the very pattern and measure of all he was to demand: just to *be* somewhere—almost anywhere would do—and somehow receive an impression or an accession, feel a relation or a vibration." [6]

When the Civil War broke out, the family had recently returned from Europe and settled in Newport, R. I. Henry's two younger brothers were soon to join the Union Army, but Henry was incapacitated by a back injury that he had sustained in fighting a fire. The injury kept him prostrate for several hours a day for years. One consequence was that invalidism plays a large part in his fiction, most notably in the sickly but appealing form of Ralph Touchett in *The Portrait of a Lady*. Though he was kept from the army, James felt that he had to join something, so, in what was ever afterwards to remain for him an inexplicable decision, he went to Cambridge in the fall of 1862 and

[4] R. N. Foley, *Criticism in American Periodicals of the Works of Henry James from 1865 to 1916* (Washington, D.C., 1944), 28.

[5] *The Letters of Henry James*, ed. Percy Lubbock (New York, 1920), I, 91.

[6] *A Small Boy and Others* (New York, 1913), 25.

enrolled in the Harvard Law School. There has probably never been a law student so inept, but James, surrounded for the first time by countrymen his own age, did feel that he was at last associated with "matters normally, entirely, consistently American. . . ." [7] He dropped out of the law school after a session of a moot court, where he found himself up before the crowd of his peers, his mouth gaping, without a thing in his head to say. In Cambridge, however, he did find the time and solitude in which to launch out on his literary career: he published his first story, anonymously, in February, 1864.

James was to serve a long apprenticeship before his work took on particular individuality. This was partly because his early life had given him little sense of local or national experience, the ground in which most authors sow their first seeds. More than most writers, James's perceptions were formed by his reading, first of English authors and then of French. Most of his early efforts were attempts to fit American experience into the framework of French and British models. A good example of this is "Poor Richard." The title comes from Ben Franklin's almanac, but the amorous theme and passionate manner of the tale are taken from the romances of George Sand. Leon Edel, James's biographer, has shown how the story's situation was based on Henry's own experience. In the summer of 1865, with the war recently over, Henry went for a vacation to North Conway in the White Mountains of New Hampshire. With him were two friends, Oliver Wendell Holmes, Jr., and John Gray, who were both later to distinguish themselves in the practice and teaching of law. Holmes and Gray had recently been demobilized from the Union Army and were still wearing their officer's uniforms. Also staying in North Conway were some cousins of Henry called the Temples, including Minnie, a beautiful, brilliant girl who was to die tragically in her early twenties. The two soldiers and the civilian revolved around Minnie, the heroine of the drama, as he called her later in his autobiography. Beside the bronzed, vigorous, and articulate veterans and the vivacious Minnie, Henry felt awkward and inadequate. This sense of frustration he expressed in "Poor Richard," in which the immature and temperamental Richard competes with two Union officers for the hand of the heroine. James was to use a similar situation when he wrote *The Portrait of a Lady* fifteen years later. In the novel, four suitors revolve around Isabel, and the disabled one, Ralph, seems to be quite closely identified with James himself. The portrait of Isabel is drawn in part from Minnie who, granted all the potentialities of life, was imprisoned by death, just as Isabel is imprisoned by her marriage. James was particularly haunted by the fact that Minnie,

[7] *Notes of a Son and Brother* (New York, 1914), 303.

shortly before her death, was planning to go to Europe for the first time. In *The Portrait of a Lady,* James was, in a sense, granting her in fiction the extra lease on life and experience that she was never to have in fact. Even that imaginary representation was not to exorcise her lambent spirit for James. Much later he was once again "to seek to lay the ghost by wrapping it, a particular occasion aiding, in the beauty and dignity of art." [8] The resulting novel, *The Wings of the Dove,* is in many ways the cap and perfection of James's art.

After the Civil War, Henry James went to Europe twice. On his return each time, he tried to settle down and write in the United States. He wanted above all to be an American novelist, but, try as he might, he could not rest content in a civilization that appeared to him to be thin and provincial in its private life and crude and corrupt in its public. He finally concluded that it took an old civilization to set a novelist in motion and, regretfully leaving his family and friends, he went in 1875 to settle in Paris. It turned out that Paris did not agree with him either; the French writers were, he thought, too limited and selfishly interested in their own concerns. In 1876 he moved to London, where he was to live, except for regular visits to France and Italy, for the next twenty years of his life. After he had settled in England, his production of works of fiction, reviews, and essays rapidly increased. He soon became, and remained to the end of his life, the most prolific major author that the United States has ever produced.

His first long novel, *Roderick Hudson* (1875), was written on the subject in which he was to make his reputation and do his best work: the international theme. The archetypal pattern of this theme is as follows: the innocent American discovers Europe; he is captivated by its charm but deluded by its evil; seeking something—freedom, knowledge, marriage—he finds instead betrayal, entrapment, or death. The theme is a modern version of the fall of Adam and his exile from paradise and James was to create within this simple schema the complex patterns for dozens of novels and stories. In *Roderick Hudson,* the sculptor from Northampton, Mass., seeks to perfect his art in Rome and ends as a suicide. In *The American* (1877), Christopher Newman, the rich Californian, seeks an aristocratic wife in Paris, and is confronted at the end with the blankness of the convent wall behind which his ex-fiancée has been compelled to immure herself. In *Daisy Miller* (1879), the girl from Schenectady refuses to do what the Romans do, is snubbed by the Europeanized American young man whom she admires, and dies after recklessly exposing herself to malarial mosquitoes in the Coliseum late at night. James's little book, *Hawthorne* (1879), was in large part an analysis of a novelist who had somehow to do without Europe for most of his creative life, and who

[8] *Notes of a Son and Brother,* 515.

found it too much for his imagination when he finally reached there. Many shorter pieces that James wrote at this time also deal with the encounters of Americans with Europe. In none of them did west meet east on mutually satisfactory grounds.

Early in 1880, James began *The Portrait of a Lady,* which was serialized simultaneously in *Macmillan's Magazine* in London and the *Atlantic Monthly* in Boston. From the beginning, he was determined that it was going to be a big novel in every sense of the word. "It is from that I myself shall pretend to date," he wrote a friend, "on that I shall take my stand." [9] The novel ran its leisurely course through fourteen installments and was published in book form in both countries at the completion of serialization. Many critics have recognized *The Portrait of a Lady* as the end of James's first period as a novelist. After this, he was to investigate new forms and ideas, abandon the international theme for other subjects, and, for a time, devote himself with disastrous results to writing for the stage.

It was not until the end of the century that he was to return to the international theme to write the three great novels of his major phase, *The Ambassadors, The Wings of the Dove,* and *The Golden Bowl.* A trip to the United States, the first in over twenty years, produced the extraordinary travel book *The American Scene* (1907). The death of his brother, William, in 1910, prompted him to begin his autobiographical volumes, *A Small Boy and Others, Notes of a Son and Brother,* and the incomplete *The Middle Years.* When the Great War broke out, he was working on yet another international novel, *The Ivory Tower.* It is the story of a young man returning from Europe to the America he had left as a child to confront the consequences of inheriting an immense fortune made by one of the robber barons, his uncle. James, deeply shocked by the War and its betrayal of the kind of civilization that he had always been trying to create in and by his novels, abandoned *The Ivory Tower* before its completion. He took up another, *The Sense of the Past,* in which a young American comes to England, inherits a house, and somehow moves back a hundred years into the past to re-enact a drama that an ancestor lived through. This was also left unfinished when Henry James died in 1916. Joseph Conrad most effectively summed up his friend and mentor's achievement when he wrote in an appreciation of his work: "A novelist is a historian, the preserver, the keeper, the expounder of human experience. As is meet for a man of his descent and tradition, Mr. Henry James is the historian of fine consciences." [10]

---

[9] Quoted by Leon Edel in his introduction to *The Portrait of a Lady* (Boston, 1956), viii.

[10] In *Henry James: A Collection of Critical Essays,* ed. Leon Edel (Englewood Cliffs, N.J., 1963), 15.

There is scarcely a finer conscience in all fiction than that of Isabel Archer. She belongs in that great gallery of women of world literature who have *lived* intensely—women like Shakespeare's Cleopatra, Richardson's Pamela, Jane Austen's Emma Woodhouse, Flaubert's Emma Bovary, Tolstoy's Anna Karenina, and George Eliot's Dorothea Brooke. These are characters so vitally at the center of their fictional world that they become part of the landscape of the reader's mind. The literary tradition to which Isabel and her story belong springs undoubtedly from the sentimental form invented by Samuel Richardson in *Pamela,* in which the innocent and good heroine is betrayed by the smooth villain. Isabel herself, however, has more affinities with intellectual heroines like Dorothea Brooke. The reader experiences the analytical consciousness of these women rather than sharing their emotional vicissitudes, as he does with earlier heroines. In writers with the skill of George Eliot and James, the drama of consciousness is just as exciting to the aroused reader as the drama of emotional action.

In 1947, Professors F. O. Matthiessen and Kenneth Murdock published *The Notebooks of Henry James* that had been deposited by the James family in the Houghton Library at Harvard. *The Notebooks* have proved a splendid mine for scholars of James and of the craft of fiction in general. From the beginning of his career, James was a remarkably self-conscious artist, and it is often possible to follow the course of one of his novels from the first germ of the idea through successive stages of working out up to a full scenario of the plot. The first entry or entries on *The Portrait of a Lady,* however, must have been made in a notebook that did not survive. The first entry that we have occurs after the novel had begun its serialization and shows James working out refinements and conclusions rather than outlines and developments. Only one comprehensive statement of his intention remains: "The idea of the whole thing is that the poor girl, who has dreamed of freedom and nobleness, who has done, as she believes, a generous, natural, clear-sighted thing, finds herself in reality ground in the very mill of the conventional." [11] Twenty-five years later, in the preface written for the revised edition of the novel, James did, however, recall how he first conceived of *The Portrait.* It began for him, he wrote, not in an idea for a plot, but "in a sense of a character, the character and aspect of a particular engaging young woman. . . ." Given that character, he was then faced with the question of what he facetiously called "positively organizing an ado about Isabel Archer." James confessed to having no recollection of how the other characters made their way into his scheme. It may be that he had unconsciously suppressed the awkward little drama in the White Mountains that

[11] *The Notebooks of Henry James,* ed. F. O. Matthiessen and Kenneth B. Murdock (New York, 1947), 15.

took place fifteen years before he wrote the novel. According to his preface, "it was as if the other characters had simply, by an impulse of their own, floated into my ken, and all in response to my primary question: 'Well, what will she do?' " [12]

The plot followed its logical course from this confrontation of Isabel with the various aspects of her destiny as they took shape in the carefully contrasted American, British, and expatriate suitors. James built his novel carefully. Later he thought it, next to *The Ambassadors*, architecturally the best of all his productions. His main problem was how to present the action of the story. He found the answer to this problem in a remark by George Eliot about women in life and fiction: "In these frail vessels is borne onward through the ages the treasure of human affection." Isabel was, James noted, "a weak agent"—and surely he had in mind far more than the usual Victorian stress on "the weaker sex." The easy way out of the problem of showing her weakness and strength lay in presenting her from the vantage point of the other characters. James decided against this method. " 'Place the centre of the subject in the young woman's consciousness,' I said to myself, 'and you get as interesting and as beautiful a difficulty as you would wish.' " [13]

It was in Isabel's sense of her own adventures that James sought to locate the drama of the novel. He thought later that he had best succeeded in doing this in Chapter Forty-two, in which Isabel sits alone by the dying fire and goes back over her recent life. Small wonder that the older James was to regard this chapter as the triumph of the book, for it foreshadowed the kind of work that he was to do in his later years—the intense analysis of consciousness. It must be said, however, that James, in his preface, was glossing over one of the most important narrative devices in the novel. Although it is true to say that the center of his subject lies in Isabel's consciousness, James in his *persona* of omniscient author, is frequently intruding on his work.

The convention of the omniscient narrator is almost as old as English fiction itself. Fielding, Dickens, Thackeray, to mention only the most eminent, genially spoke up in their novels to instruct and divert their "gentle readers." Even when absent in the first person they and almost all other eighteenth and nineteenth century novelists took the liberty of introducing their readers freely to the minds of any or all of the characters. In *The Portrait* James did not avail himself so much of the latter privilege as he did of the former. As narrator, he is often nudging his reader into judgment of or indulgence to his heroine. Later in his career, he was to abjure this kind of manipulation, and seek to make his novels fully dramatic and analytic, with extensive

[12] *The Novels and Tales of Henry James* (New York, 1908), III, xvii.
[13] *The Novels and Tales of Henry James*, III, xv.

reporting from inside either one central or three or four major characters. With this new technique, he was to lay the groundwork for the
rise of the modern novel as it has been written by Joyce, Virginia
Woolf, Faulkner, Camus, and many others.

But in writing *The Portrait* James was still influenced by the powerful conventions of the novel of his time. He mentions two authors
in the preface who had a particular effect on his work. The first was
Turgenieff, whom he had come to know well during his year in Paris.
The expatriate Russian author confided to his young American friend
that his own fictions usually originated in a character or characters for
whom he then had to find a subject. This encouraged James to proceed in a similar way; indeed it confirmed, with great authority, his
own inclinations. James was influenced by Turgenieff in several ways,
as Daniel Lerner has shown.[14] In the resistant, individualistic nature
of Turgenieff's Russian heroines, James saw a clue to the treatment of
his American women. Turgenieff also insisted on the importance of
architecture in the novel and probably influenced James not only in
the way that he structured the novel so carefully, but also in the
pervasive use of architectural metaphors and symbols in *The Portrait
of a Lady*. It seems likely also that Turgenieff's vivid sense of the tex-
ture of life, particularly its movement, color, and smell, helped to
shape James's perception.

The other, equally important influence mentioned by James in his
preface is George Eliot. F. R. Leavis has discussed the subject in *The
Great Tradition*. Another critic, George Levine, has considerably am-
plified Leavis' discussion.[15] He takes account not only of what James
learned from Eliot, but also how he transcended her vision. He points
out that James drew more inspiration from Dorothea Brooke of *Middlemarch* (1872) than any other heroine of George Eliot. Both Isabel
and Dorothea are intellectual and theoretical by nature. Like Dorothea,
Isabel chooses to marry a man who does not fit conventional patterns
and finds herself trapped in the conventional. Both recognize their
fault in the choice of partners. But whereas Dorothea's story is seen
against the larger social backdrop of the society of *Middlemarch,* Isabel's story is purely hers. By his technique, James concentrates on his
heroine's life and almost entirely ignores the larger social and historical
world in which his characters presumably live. Moreover, James follows his heroine's actions through to their bitter consequences. Isabel,
at the end, faces her bleak future. George Eliot's vision, on the other
hand, is dispersed among the various members of her fictional society,

[14] Daniel Lerner, "The Influence of Turgenev on Henry James," *Slavonic Review*
XX (Dec., 1941), 28–54.
[15] George Levine, "Isabel, Gwendolen, and Dorothea," *Journal of English Literary
History* XXX (Sept., 1963), 244–57.

and she does not feel obliged to see each case through to its conclusion. She lets Dorothea off the hook of fate by killing off her husband. Her Victorian vision of social meliorism apparently inhibited her from implementing in her novel the bitter fact that mistakes in life are usually irrevocable.

James's concentration on the lonely fate of the individual brings us to another equally important consideration of the background to *The Portrait of a Lady*—the American influences. Richard Chase's essay analyzes James's debt to the romance tradition of the American novel, and R. W. Stallman discusses some aspects of the particular influence of Hawthorne. Perhaps it is enough to add here how prominent has been the role of the isolated hero in American fiction—from James Fenimore Cooper's Natty Bumppo to Truman Capote's Holly Golightly. The most obvious predecessor of Isabel in American fiction is Hester Prynne of *The Scarlet Letter*. At the end of the novel she, like Isabel, refuses the easy way out and chooses to return to the town where she had made her original decision and live out its consequences. The American hero, unlike his British counterpart, refuses to be identified with or by his society, and therefore does not seek compromises with it. The most important exchange of ideas in *The Portrait of a Lady* is between Madame Merle, the image of European social adaptability, and Isabel. " 'One's self,' " Madame Merle says, " '—for other people—is one's expression of one's self; and one's house, one's furniture, one's garments, the books one reads, the company one keeps—these things are all expressive.' " Isabel replies: " 'I think just the other way. I don't know whether I succeed in expressing myself, but I know that nothing expresses me. Nothing that belongs to me is any measure of me; everything's on the contrary a limit, a barrier, and a perfectly arbitrary one.' " Part of Isabel's moral education in Europe is to learn to modify that individualistic doctrine, to find out that freedom is always subject to conditions.

In writing *The Portrait of a Lady*, James drew on many more sources, as Oscar Cargill has shown.[16] The variety of this background is reflected in the mixed nature of the novel's form. Primarily, it is written according to the conventions of realism that James had learned from French writers like Balzac and Flaubert as well as George Eliot, Anthony Trollope, and Charles Dickens. But the romance elements of the American tradition deeply influence the nature of the story. I have mentioned already the analogy between Isabel's story and the story of Adam's exile from Paradise, which is, as R. W. B. Lewis has shown, perhaps the archetypal American romance form.[17] Another romance element in *The Portrait* is the awakening of the sleeping beauty. Isa-

[16] Oscar Cargill, *The Novels of Henry James* (New York, 1961), 78–97.
[17] *The American Adam* (Chicago, 1955), 152–55.

bel's European experience awakens her to the richness and complexity of life, as well as to its evil. The one kiss mentioned in the novel—at the very end—awakens her in another way, to the power of sexuality, which she rejects in fleeing back inside the house of Gardencourt. Ironically, too, the action of the novel can be viewed as a version of another fairy tale: of the poor girl who winds up as a princess living in a castle. So skillfully does James handle these romance elements, however, that we do not sense them as being obtrusively unreal within the carefully planned sequence of realistic cause and effect of the novel's plot.

When James wrote the notebook entry for *The Portrait of a Lady* that was mentioned earlier, he accurately prophesied the criticisms that would be made of his novel. "The weakness of the whole story," he wrote, "is that it is too exclusively psychological—that it depends too little on incident." [18] He planned to make up this defect in the second half of the novel, but it may be questioned whether or not he did. James knew that the audience he was writing for, brought up on the fiction of Scott, Dickens, Thackeray, and the other great storytellers of the nineteenth century, might expect more action, and it is certain that some of his twentieth century readers expect it too. In James's mature novels, however, very little *happens*. All the same the attentive reader of James's novel, once he has accustomed himself to the leisurely pace, can find many other sources of interest.

James's prose style is in itself worth the closest attention. By today's standards it is of course indirect, complicated, polysyllabic, and stately. But a closer look reveals that it is often being used for wonderful comic purposes; it is often used to mock the foibles and pretensions of the characters, the reader, and even the narrator himself. Take for example the discussion of Mrs. Touchett's telegram in Chapter One. Ralph obviously knows perfectly well what it means, but he plays with the message in his typically droll way and illuminates at the same time the character of his mother. *The Portrait of a Lady* is one of the finest comedies of international manners in existence, and its wit is underscored by one of the sharpest senses of irony since Jane Austen. James's style is also highly poetic. It is full of devices that we normally expect to find in verse rather than prose. Examine, for example, the patterns of alliteration, euphony, and assonance that occur in a sentence in the first paragraph of the book. "Real dusk would not arrive for many hours; but the flood of summer light had begun to ebb, the air had grown mellow, the shadows were long upon the smooth, dense turf. They lengthened slowly, however, and the scene expressed that sense of leisure still to come which is perhaps the chief source of one's enjoy-

[18] *Notebooks*, 15.

ment of such a scene at such an hour." Like much good poetry, too, James's prose is full of images, often expressed in metaphor and simile. When he revised his text for the New York Edition (the one almost invariably used for today's reprints), he created many new images as well as extending old ones. A good example occurs in his summary of his discussion of Ralph's ill-health. In the first edition, James wrote: "The truth was that he had simply accepted the situation." The revision reads: "His serenity was but the array of wild flowers niched in his ruin." In addition to creating a vivid little picture for the reader's mind, James, by this change, commented succinctly on Ralph's attitude towards life.

Unlike most novelists, James did not reveal character in action so much as in conversation and description. The description is rich with patterns of imagery which enlarge and define character. Goodwood, for example, is given many images of chivalry and military force; Henrietta is characterized by images of publicity and printing presses, and so on. In his preface, James remarked that he had overdone Henrietta. She was, he thought, a product of youthful zeal and "a part of my wonderful notion of the lively." [19] But we would not willingly see less of her in the novel, nor of the ineffable Mr. Bantling whom Henrietta incongruously marries. In fact the minor characters of *The Portrait*, from Pansy to the Countess Gemini, are sketched in as bright vignettes, and yet are at the same time psychologically convincing and structurally necessary.

James foresaw another criticism that would be made of his novel. It would, he thought, appear to some to be unfinished because he had "not seen the heroine to the end of her situation." He supplied his own answer to that criticism on the spot. "The *whole* of anything is never told; you can only take what groups together. What I have done has that unity—it groups together." [20] Sure enough, many reviewers made precisely this criticism. The first edition gave them some warrant for believing the novel to be incomplete. It ended with Caspar Goodwood calling on Henrietta in London to ask after Isabel. She tells him that Isabel has already left for Rome. Then she says: " 'Look here, Mr. Goodwood . . . just you wait.' " And the first edition ends with the words: "On which he looked up at her." In his revision James indicated that the reader was not to trust Henrietta's characteristically facile optimism. After "looked up at her," he added, "—but only to guess, from her face with a revulsion, that she simply meant he was young. She stood shining at him with that cheap comfort, and it added, on the spot, thirty years to his life. She walked him away with her,

[19] *The Novels and Tales of Henry James*, III, xxi.
[20] *Notebooks*, 18.

however, as if she had given him the key to patience." The new ending did not, however, suppress debate on the meaning of the conclusion. I have included in this volume some of the work done on this
question. In a sense, though, what lies beyond those last words is im-
material to *The Portrait of a Lady*. The picture is beautifully complete; what lies outside the frame is no business of the artist. James
himself had the last word on this artistic problem. In his preface to
Roderick Hudson he wrote: "Really, universally, relations stop nowhere, and the exquisite problem of the artist is eternally but to draw,
by a geometry of his own, the circle within which they shall happily
appear to do so." [21]

The reasons for Isabel's decision to return to her husband do not
take us beyond the book's conclusion but back to its contents. I would
stress only one aspect of the meaning of Isabel's return to Osmond.
Partly because of his own temperament and partly because of the
reticence of the publishers of the time, James did not spell out the sexual elements of his situation. All the same, he knew perfectly well
what he was doing, and it would be a mistake to assume that he was
not aware of the sexual coldness of Isabel Archer (whose surname
suggests the chaste Diana, goddess of the hunt). As her most sym-
pathetic but most acute critic, Ralph, remarks to her: "You want to
see, but not to feel." Isabel is a true descendant of the Puritans, whose
distrust of emotions led them to rely too much on the analyzing intel-
lect. She shies away from the sexuality in Lord Warburton and particularly in Caspar Goodwood. She commits herself to Osmond at least
in part because he is a "sterile dilettante," as Ralph calls him, and
offers no sexual threat. It seems to me that through this theme in the
novel, James is making not only an evaluation of his heroine but also
a criticism of the effect that American life has on some of its citizens in
suppressing and distorting natural sexuality. Hawthorne often treated
the same theme in his fiction.

In its largest sense *The Portrait of a Lady* is the story of an encounter between two civilizations, American and European. James was accurately prefiguring cultural encounters that have since taken place
between Americans and representatives from other cultures all over
the world. Many of Isabel's compatriots have shared and still
share her innocence, her emotional coldness, and her slightly chau-
vinistic confidence and pride. In *The Quiet American,* Graham
Greene, a close student of James's work, has shown what happens when
such qualities meet an Asiatic culture. Written in 1955 and set in Viet-
nam, the novel accurately predicted the pattern of subsequent tragic
events. The difference between Isabel's America and Pyle's America is

---

[21] *The Novels and Tales of Henry James* (New York, 1907), I, vii.

that the years between their publications saw the United States emerge from a provincial country to the world's greatest power. Isabel's faults could lead to little more than her personal tragedy; today, as Greene's novel shows, those same faults can lead to actions that are nothing less than global in their effects.

The Lesson of the Master

by Richard Chase

Henry James's *Portrait of a Lady* (1880) was the first novel by an American that made, within the limits of its subject, full use of the novel form. By comparison, no previous American novel, even those of James, can claim to be fully "done." From James's point of view the older American romance-novelists had many faults. Some of these he singles out explicitly in his biography of Hawthorne, others he directly or indirectly deals with in his prefaces and critical writings. Cooper, Hawthorne, and Melville (actually James seems to know next to nothing of the last) relied too readily on extravagant events and startling characters. They failed to render experience fully. They failed to illustrate and dramatize connections and relations. They did not see (in the words of the Preface to *Roderick Hudson*) that for the true novelist "the continuity of things is the whole matter . . . of comedy and tragedy."

To read the first page of *The Portrait of a Lady* is to step into a world unfrequented by the earlier American novelists. A handsome pictorial representation, a fine old house, beautiful lawns and gardens, a group of people being set in motion—all these may be found in Cooper's *Satanstoe* or Hawthorne's *House of the Seven Gables*. But James's procedure is different from that of the earlier writers. The effect he seeks is more organic and self-contained. At the same time, there is more detail, more careful observation, for he has "researched" his subject—something which Hawthorne, as James said, tended to leave undone. We encounter at the very beginning the author's reference to his book as a "history" and we are perhaps reminded that in his essay "The Art of Fiction" (1884) he was to say that the novel should give the same impression of veracity as does history itself.

On the broad, sloping lawn of the mansion James calls Garden-

"The Lesson of the Master." From The American Novel and Its Tradition *by Richard Chase (New York: Doubleday & Company, Inc., 1957), pp. 117–35. Copyright © 1957 by Richard Chase. Reprinted by permission of the publisher.*

court we discover people taking tea, and they are finding it agreeable, not only because it tastes good but because drinking it is a mild ritual by which they show themselves to be a part of a way of life, a social order which we understand is to figure strongly in the book, as strongly as does the life of the Westchester aristocracy in *Satanstoe*. Yet the life of James's characters will be illustrated and dramatized with a far more exact and also a more poetic art than one can find in Cooper's novel.

To admit, as most readers would, that there is an element of poetry in *The Portrait of a Lady* is to admit that though it has all of the novelistic virtues, it has others too. There is a sense in which one might speak of the "poetry" of *Pride and Prejudice* or *Middlemarch*— a poetry of picture and scene, a poetry felt to belong to the organized effect of character, action, and setting. But this is, so to speak, novelistic poetry, of the kind every interesting novel has. *The Portrait* has it too, but it also has a further dimension of poetry, to understand which one must perceive that James's novel is akin to romance as the others are not.

It is an important fact about James's art that he gave up what he considered the claptrap of romance without giving up its mystery and beauty. Mr. Leavis in *The Great Tradition* is not interested in James as a romancer, but he nevertheless notes that James is a "poet-novelist" and says that he combines Jane Austen's skill of observing and dramatizing manners with Hawthorne's "profoundly moral and psychological . . . poetic art of fiction." This is very well put, and it supports the supposition of this chapter that a part of James's great program for improving the novel consisted of the reconstitution, on new grounds, of romance. Often one has difficulty in pinning down any one element of a James novel as belonging to romance because the author has so completely subdued and transmuted it to suit his exacting novelistic purposes. The element of romance becomes generally subverted and assimilated; yet in turn it imparts the glow of poetry to the realistic substance of the novel. Which is to say in a different way what Mr. Leavis says in the following: "James's own constant and profound concern with spiritual facts expresses itself not only in what obviously demands to be called symbolism, but in the handling of character, episode, and dialogue, and in the totality of the plot, so that when he seems to offer a novel of manners, he gives us more than that and the 'poetry' is major."

The conscious assimilation of romance into the novelistic substance of *The Portrait* took place in two different ways. It was assimilated into the language of the book and produced a general enrichment of metaphor. It was also brought in in the character of Isabel Archer, the heroine, who is to a considerable extent our point of view as we read. Isabel tends to see things as a romancer does, whereas the author sees things with the firmer, more comprehensive, and more disillusioned vision of the novelist. Thus James brings the element of romance into the novel in such a way that he can both share in the romantic point of view of his heroine and separate himself from it by taking an objective view of it.

The metaphors of *The Portrait of a Lady* do not often rival the amazingly elaborate figures one encounters in James's later works, but by contrast with the usual practice of the novel at the time James wrote they are notably daring—so much so that sometimes they seem to lead a life of their own within the spacious world of the book, although in each case we are led to see the relevance of the metaphor to the course of events and to the pattern of unfolding significance. There is a paradox, says James in his Preface to *The Portrait,* in trying to write a fiction at once so complex and so ambitious. The paradox is that a novel so conceived must "positively . . . appear more true to its character in proportion as it strains, or tends to burst, with a latent extravagance, its mould." Metaphor offered to James a kind of repository or annex in which the latent extravagance of his imagination might take form. As has often been noticed the main figures of speech in James's novel—although the variety is rich—have to do with the house and the garden.

The metaphors are sometimes extravagant. For example we read of Isabel that "her imagination was by habit ridiculously active; when the door was not open it jumped out of the window." But that is a mere piece of fancy and reminds us less of the characteristic practice of James than of the quaint wit of Hawthorne. Ordinarily, James's metaphors, in *The Portrait* as elsewhere, are not quaint and concise. They are suggestively imaginative and they are likely to be given a tone of elevated levity which at once enjoys what is being said and takes note of its extravagance. As often as not the Jamesian metaphor shows that mixture of serious poetic imagination with humor which we find in other American writers, notably Melville, Mark Twain, and Faulkner. Although one would hardly mistake the style of any one of these writers for that of any other, all of them are fond of the serious, intricately sustained joke. Here is James speaking of Ralph Touchett's pose of facetious irony, which Isabel, in her earnest sincerity, finds baffling and also reprehensible. Sensing his inner despair and sorry that he is sickly, she wants to come directly to the "real" Ralph Touchett, but he himself explains the value of his pose:

> "I keep a band of music in my ante-room. It has orders to play without stopping; it renders me two excellent services. It keeps the sounds of the world from reaching the private apartments, and it makes the world think that dancing's going on within." It was dance music indeed that you

usually heard when you came within earshot of Ralph's band; the liveliest waltzes seemed to float upon the air. Isabel often found herself irritated by this perpetual fiddling; she would have liked to pass—

James finds the metaphor, once launched, too good to drop—

through the ante-room, as her cousin called it, and enter the private apartments. It mattered little that he had assured her they were a very dismal place; she would have been glad to undertake to sweep them and set them in order. It was but half-hospitality to let her remain outside.

The idea of leaving and entering a house, the contrast of different kinds of houses, the question of whether a house is a prison or the scene of liberation and fulfillment—these are the substance of the metaphors in *The Portrait of a Lady*. Figuratively speaking, the story told in the novel is of Isabel's leaving an American house—a way of life, that is—for a European house. Ostensibly she conceives of this as an escape from frustrating and cramping confinement to a fuller, freer, more resonant and significant life. Actually, it is not hard to see that although James has much admiration and tenderness of feeling for his heroine, he gives her an element of perverse Yankee idealism of the sort that he was shortly to portray in the more exacerbated form of positively per*verted* idealism in Olive Chancellor in *The Bostonians*. So that for all her dark-haired, gray-eyed beauty, her delightful young enthusiasm, and her zest for life, there is in Isabel a fatal susceptibility to a form of imprisonment worse than that she has escaped. Figuratively, the house in which she lives as the wife of Gilbert Osmond confines her in a hopeless imprisonment she could not consciously have imagined.

Our first sight of Isabel occurs when with her abrupt charm and her disarming candor she walks across the lawn at Gardencourt, the Touchetts' English estate, and presents herself to her cousin Ralph, his father, and Lord Warburton. But then in the form of a flash-back we are speedily acquainted with the general circumstances of Isabel's childhood and girlhood. We find her in the old family house at Albany talking with Mrs. Touchett and greeting with joy Mrs. Touchett's offer to take her to Europe. "To go to Florence," says Isabel, "I'd promise almost anything!" She sees in this offer an escape from the loneliness of the life she has known in the great, empty, dismal house. Yet now that escape is in view, Isabel admits that she does not hate the house or the circumstances of her early life, even though Mrs. Touchett dismisses the place as "very bourgeois." "I like places in which things have happened," says Isabel, "—even if they're sad things. A great many people have died here; the place has been full of life." And to Mrs. Touchett's query "Is that what you call being full of life?" she replies, "I mean full of experience—of people's feelings and sorrows. And not of their sorrows only, for I've been happy here as a child."

Still, the possibility of living a full life in Albany seems remote to Isabel. And the only considerable picture of her as a young girl that James gives us suggests that she had found the Albany house not so much the scene of human sufferings and joys as the somewhat bleak abode of a life of fantasy and reading, a life isolated from reality. Isabel had been accustomed to read and daydream in a room known as "the office" that lay beyond the library.

> The place owed much of its mysterious melancholy to the fact that it was properly entered from the second door of the house, the door that had been condemned, and that it was secured by bolts which a particularly slender little girl found it impossible to slide. She knew that this silent, motionless portal opened into the street; if the sidelights had not been filled with green paper she might have looked out upon the little brown stoop and the well-worn brick pavement. But she had no wish to look out, for this would have interfered with her theory that there was a strange, unseen place on the other side—a place which became to the child's imagination, according to its different moods, a region of delight or terror.

She is sitting in this room when Mrs. Touchett comes to see her, except that being now a young woman with undefined but strong purposes she is, on this fateful afternoon, not engaging in childish fantasy but, having given her mind "marching orders," she has sent it "trudging over the sandy plains of a history of German thought."

Despite her disorganized and tenuous education and the puritanism of her native Yankee temperament, Isabel is now ostensibly ready to pursue an enriched life of the emotions and of thought. A way of life characterized by its intricate amenity, its depth of emotion, and its richness of traditionally ordered experience cannot be symbolized by the house at Albany. But it can by the Tudor mansion of the Touchetts, to which Isabel is introduced when she arrives in England.

> Her uncle's house seemed a picture made real; no refinement of the agreeable was lost on Isabel: the rich perfection of Gardencourt at once revealed a world and gratified a need. The deep embrasures and curious casements, the quiet light on dark polished panels, the deep greenness outside, that seemed always peeping in, the sense of a well-ordered privacy in the centre of a "property"—a place where sounds were felicitously accidental, where the tread was muffled by the earth itself and in the thick mild air all friction dropped out of contact and all shrillness out of talk . . .

There is no paper in the windows of this house, no need to isolate oneself from the world outside. On the contrary the "greenness outside" seems "always peeping in" and the garden, where at important points in the novel Isabel will receive and reject proposals of marriage from Lord Warburton and Caspar Goodwood, seems as much a part of the house as does its own interior. Consequently, the garden makes an inevitable part of the general metaphor which represents the enriched sensibility of the heroine.

> She was always planning out her development, desiring her perfection, observing her progress. Her nature had, in her conceit, a certain garden-like quality, a suggestion of perfume and murmuring boughs, of shady bowers and lengthening vistas, which made her feel that introspection was, after all, an exercise in the open air, and that a visit to the recesses of one's spirit was harmless when one returned from it with a lapful of roses.

In a novel which describes a fall from innocence, it is suitable that the tragic action should be metaphorically mirrored in the heroine's mind by this imaginative conjunction of the garden and the ancient house, in which the garden stands for Isabel's Eve-like innocence and the house for a civilization that has lost its innocence but has acquired —along with its corruption—wisdom, maturity, and the whole involved and valuable accretion of culture. Thus Isabel is akin not only to the heroines of George Eliot, such as Hetty Sorrel, Maggie Tulliver, Rosamond Vincy, and Gwendolen Harleth, with whom James compares her in his Preface; nor is she akin only to Shakespeare's Portia, with whom James also compares Isabel, calling Portia "the very type and model of the young person intelligent and presumptuous." Isabel also resembles the strong-minded Rosalind in *As You Like It* and the innocent and expectant Miranda in *The Tempest.* And the particular charm of these girls is that they are "real," that they make positive demands on life, but that they are at the same time figures of romance. James is also thinking of the Miltonic archetype of all feminine innocence, as is suggested by his using, as Leon Edel points out, the language of *Paradise Lost* to describe Isabel as she sets out on her adventures: "The world lay before her—she could do whatever she chose."

Chapter 42 of *The Portrait* brings to its fullest realization, though not to its last refinement, the characteristic art of James, that art which I am attempting to define as an assimilation of romance into the substance of the novel. James describes this chapter by saying that, "It is obviously the best thing in the book, but it is only a supreme illustration of the general plan." In this chapter James was able to achieve supremely the "circuit" of the real and the ideal, of action and fantasy, and thus to capture along with the realistic substance of the story the wonder and beauty of romance while at the same time rejecting the conventional devices of romance.

Isabel, now the wife of Osmond, sits one evening by the fire in the drawing room of Osmond's house, and with a combination of disillusioned insight and darkly working imagination she recognizes for the first time the true character of her husband and the true nature of her predicament. The problem, as James sees it, is how to present an episode in which nothing happens except an "extraordinary meditative vigil" but which will have all the excitement of action and high adventure. The problem is how to make the "mystic conversion" of Isabel's adventures, which have actually been "mild," into "the stuff of drama," how, as he goes on to say, to produce "the maximum of intensity with the minimum of strain." The "circuit" of the real and the fantasied, the "mystic conversion" of which James speaks, is to be established not, certainly, through a mere retelling or summing-up of Isabel's "mild adventures," but by giving us her sense of them. "Without her sense of them, her sense *for* them, as one may say, they are next to nothing at all." Although there are no overt happenings in this chapter, it nevertheless, as James says, "throws the action further forward than twenty 'incidents' might have done. It was designed to have all the vivacity of incident and all the economy of picture. Isabel sits up, by her dying fire, far into the night, under the spell of recognitions on which she finds the last sharpness suddenly wait. It is a representation simply of her motionlessly *seeing*, and an attempt withal to make the mere still lucidity of her act as 'interesting' as the surprise of a caravan or the identification of a pirate."

What occurs in Isabel's mind is the kind of disillusioned and profoundly realistic perception of truth about oneself and one's situation that is called "tragic recognition." Yet it comes to her in images that belong as much to melodrama as to tragedy. "Her soul was haunted by terrors," says James, "which crowded to the foreground of thought as quickly as a place was made for them." One of these terrors is the new image she has formed of her husband, an image which distinctly reminds us of one of the cold, selfish villains of Hawthorne, a Rappaccini or a Chillingworth. She thinks of Osmond's "faculty for making everything wither that he touched, spoiling everything for her that he looked at. . . . It was as if he had had the evil eye; as if his presence were a blight and his favor a misfortune."

She reflects that she had set out with her husband for "the high places of happiness." She had taken "all the first steps in the purest confidence," but now "she had suddenly found the infinite vista of a multiplied life to be a dark narrow alley with a dead wall at the end." The man who had so narrowed and enclosed her life, a creature of darkness, now steps forth into the light—"she had seen only half his nature then, as one saw the disk of the moon when it was partly masked by the shadow of the earth. She saw the full moon now—she saw the whole man."

But the full force of Isabel's recognition is appropriately conveyed by the metaphor of the house and the garden. She has escaped, to be sure, the isolation and girlish ignorance she had known at Albany, but she has lost the felicitous synthesis of innocence and experience sym-bolized as a possibility for her by Gardencourt. Her marriage, as she now sees, had made her the inhabitant of a different house.

> She could live it over again, the incredulous terror with which she had taken the measure of her dwelling. Between these four walls she had lived ever since; they were to surround her for the rest of her life. It was the house of darkness, the house of dumbness, the house of suffocation. Osmond's beautiful mind gave it neither light nor air; Osmond's beautiful mind indeed seemed to peep down from a small high window and mock at her.

And so Isabel comes to see that

> under all his culture, his cleverness, his amenity, under his good-nature, his facility, his knowledge of life, his egotism lay hidden like a serpent in a bank of flowers.

Her youthful innocence and good-will have been foully traduced, she has been the victim of an elegantly sordid conspiracy, the possibility of a full life she had envisioned has been spoiled. And we are left to recall, with a sense of its tragic irony, her early declaration to Lord Warburton that "I can't escape my fate"—that fate which Isabel had thought would consist of some rewarding involvement in life. For although she has rather grand aspirations, an essential stipulation of her fate, as she understands it, is that she shall never be exempt "from the usual chances and dangers, from what most people know and suffer." She has found knowledge and suffering no doubt, but of the grimmest sort. In her plight there can be no such clarion awakening and engagement of her human faculties as she had supposed might be the result of knowledge and suffering. Indeed there seems nothing left for her but a life of duty and abnegation. As we leave her at the end of the book she seems veritably to belong to the sisterhood of Hester Prynne.

But we know why Hester Prynne is made to suffer; conventional morality imposes on her its punishment for a sin of passion. For better or for worse, Isabel remains scrupulously virginal. She has been guilty of no misconduct in which we find any real justification for suffering. And we do, of course, want to find some measure of justification; otherwise we shall have to convict James of palming off on us under the guise of moral complexity what is morally speaking a mere melodrama of victimized innocence, a tale of merely senseless cruelty and pathos.

Is James himself subtly vindictive in his attitude toward Isabel? He clearly admires her for her almost redemptive American probity and moral spontaneity, and yet he just as clearly thinks her guilty of presumption, and of bad manners that are only just barely made tolerable by her ingenuous charm. Nor does James approve of her upbringing or of her father, one of those somewhat disorderly, nomadic Americans for whom he always shows a dislike. Isabel has been taught to "affront her destiny," as James says in his Preface; and this, one supposes, is less correct than *con*fronting it. Even supposing, as there is some speculative ground for doing, that James has a neurotic involvement with his heroine which leads him to fear her female aggressiveness and thus to take satisfaction and to derive a feeling of security in showing her, though possessed of animal spirits, to be sexually cold, and in leading her, finally, to her cruel fate—even supposing on these or other grounds a genuine animosity on the part of James toward his heroine, the fact remains that this is surmounted by his admiration of her and his profound sympathy with her. And in any case Isabel is so completely created a character that she lives her life independently of the approval or disapproval the author may feel toward her, whether we deduce his feeling from the novel itself or from our knowledge of his life and temperament.

Sometimes moved, as one must be, by a desire for a more earthly and simple morality than James's usually is, one wishes that Isabel Archer were more like Kate Croy of *The Wings of the Dove* or even the unpleasantly named Fleda Vetch in *The Spoils of Poynton,* girls in whom the general quality of self-assertion has a sexual component. But despite her deeply repressed sexuality, Isabel remains among the most complex, the most fully realized, and the most humanly fascinating of James's characters. Consequently we cannot think her a mere case of victimized innocence. She has so many powers, imperfect though they are, of knowledge, of feeling, of imagination that her fate must surely issue in some crucial way from her being the sort of person she is. If she is disqualified for triumph, it is not in the obvious way of James's other victimized innocents, like Catherine Sloper in *Washington Square,* who is homely and timid, like Maisie in *What Maisie Knew* or little Miles and Flora in *The Turn of the Screw,* who are children, or like Milly Theale in *The Wings of the Dove,* who is dying of tuberculosis. Isabel's disqualification is that of heroines and heroes throughout tragic literature—a blindness to reality, a distortion of awareness, that puts her at the mercy of the perverse and self-destructive inner motives struggling in her for the upper hand.

Without attempting any sort of full discussion of Isabel and her troubles, one may note that she sees reality as the romancer sees it. This is obvious as a general proposition, since Isabel is patently romantic in the sense that she has highly imaginative dreams which prove to be beyond the possibility of fulfillment. A realistic young woman, or, for that matter, a conventionally romantic one, would have accepted Lord Warburton as a good catch, for he is, after all, an excellent man as well as a rich and noble lord. But Isabel has higher ideals than any she thinks can be realized by a life with Lord Warburton. Her personal romance includes strenuous abstractions that lead her to aspire to far more than the conventional romance of marrying an English nobleman. She therefore perversely and no doubt quite mistakenly decides that to marry Lord Warburton would be to "escape" her "fate." "I can't escape unhappiness," she says. "In marrying you I shall be trying to." And she continues by saying that by marrying Lord Warburton she would be "turning away," "separating" herself from life, "from the usual chances and dangers, from what most people know and suffer." Lord Warburton's answer is one that would in the main turn out to be true: "I don't offer you any exoneration from life or from any chances or dangers whatever." He is brought by Isabel's behavior to a true understanding of her, and he exclaims, "I never saw a person judge things on such theoretic grounds." Her theory is that he is merely "a collection of attributes and powers," but this is clearly a false theory. Despite his being a hereditary nobleman and so, bound to the formalities and duties of his station in life, he presents himself to her with perfect candor as a man, and not a lord, who needs and desires her. Thus Isabel's vague democratic objections to English aristocracy, which in any case she seems generally to admire, are not the real reason why she rejects Lord Warburton. Nor when she does marry does she choose a man notable for democracy. She rejects Lord Warburton at the behest of her puritan spirituality, which leads her to flee from the mere physical and social realities of life as these would be should she marry him. Perversely and mistakenly, her argument is that marriage to Lord Warburton would exempt her from life. Better a collection of attributes and powers (which in any case Lord Warburton is not) than a collection of sterile tastes and appetites, which Gilbert Osmond certainly is. But Isabel does not see Osmond for what he is until too late. (I am assuming here as elsewhere that Isabel's choice is, for all practical purposes, between Warburton and Osmond. Ralph is in love with her, but his illness disqualifies him. The persistent Caspar Goodwood presents himself at intervals, but Isabel does not see him as an actual possibility. She seems to conceive of him as worthy but as rather stodgy in his conventional Massachusetts way. She scarcely thinks of him as being momentously on the scene until at the very end of the novel when he proposes to rescue her from Osmond and, in his vehemence, frightens her with his masculine aggressiveness by giving her, so far as the reader knows, her only kiss.)

How is it that the image Osmond presents to the world so easily commands Isabel's assent? This is a hard problem, but the answer may be suggested by observing that although Isabel's vision of things is neither that of self-interested common sense nor that of worldly romance in which poor girls marry great lords, it emphatically is that of the romance associated with the American tradition of puritanism and transcendentalism. Isabel subscribes to the American romance of the self. She believes that the self finds fulfillment either in its own isolated integrity or on a more or less transcendent ground where the contending forces of good and evil are symbolized abstractions. She sees her fate as a spiritual melodrama. Her grasp of reality, though manifold in its presumptions, is unstable, and her desire for experience is ambivalent. She rejects Lord Warburton ostensibly because she fears that marrying him will exempt her from life. But Ralph Touchett, who often speaks with the wisdom of the author, has no trouble in securing a contradictory admission from his amusing and perplexing cousin. At the end of a lengthy dialogue about her rejection of Lord Warburton, Ralph conjectures, "You want to drain the cup of experience," and gets out of Isabel this surprising answer, "No, I don't wish to touch the cup of experience. It's a poisoned drink! I only want to see for myself." To which Ralph adds a comment in the partial truth of which we may see a link between Isabel and Osmond: "You want to see, but not to feel."

Ralph has hit upon a truth about his cousin. The kind of cold, amoral aloofness, the possibly morbid passion for observing life at a distance—these are real traits of Isabel's character. True, they are no more than strong strands in her fabric. But they are strong enough so that she responds to Osmond's talk about how "one ought to make one's life a work of art," without being aware of the inhumanity and the withering aestheticism such an idea may imply. Only when it is too late does she discover the cold malignancy of her husband. Only too late does she see that, apart from his need of the money she has inherited from her uncle, she is cherished by Osmond only to the extent that he can consider her another art object in his collection. Only too late does she understand the subtle corruption that leads Osmond to try to arrange his daughter's education so as to make her life "a work of art." Listening to Osmond's plans for Pansy's schooling, Isabel seems to see at last "how far her husband's desire to be effective was capable of going—to the point of playing theoretic tricks on the delicate organism of his daughter." In this way Isabel, who is herself

every bit the theorist Lord Warburton accused her of being, comes to
understand the perverse puritan impulse which Hawthorne called
"the Unpardonable Sin." The sin is the same whether one's cold,
theoretical manipulation of others has an aesthetic motive or as with
Hawthorne's Chillingworth or Ethan Brand a quasi-scientific one.

Isabel's romance of the self, as was suggested above, requires that
self-fulfillment shall take place only at a high level of abstraction,
where the disinterested pursuit of perfection may be carried on. And
although Ralph Touchett warns his cousin that Osmond is a "sterile
aesthete," she sees in him at once the high priest, the devoted custodian,
and martyr of the life of perfection. She is very far from believing
that the ordinary vulgar circumstances of one's life have anything to
do with one's self. She finds it inconceivable and rather degrading
that anyone should suppose the self to be in any sort of dialectic with
the mere things one is surrounded by. In Chapter 19 there occurs an
important exchange between Madame Merle and Isabel on this point.
They have been talking about the inevitable "young man with a
mustache" who must figure in some way in every young woman's life.
Madame Merle speculatively inquires whether Isabel's "young man
with a mustache" has a "castle in the Apennines" or "an ugly brick
house in Fortieth Street." And when Isabel says characteristically, "I
don't care anything about his house," Madame Merle replies, "That's
very crude of you." And she continues by saying,

> There's no such thing as an isolated man or woman; we're each of us
> made up of some cluster of appurtenances. What shall we call our "self"?
> Where does it begin? Where does it end? It overflows into everything
> that belongs to us—and then it flows back again. I know a large part of
> myself is in the clothes I choose to wear. I've a great respect for *things!*
> One's self—for other people—is one's expression of one's self; and one's
> house, one's furniture, one's garments, the books one reads, the company
> one keeps—these things are all expressive.

This bit of worldly wisdom strikes Isabel as being worldly, all too
worldly, but not as being wisdom. "I don't agree with you," she says.
"I think just the other way. I don't know whether I succeed in expressing myself, but I know that nothing else expresses me. Nothing that
belongs to me is any measure of me; everything's on the contrary a
limit, a barrier, and a perfectly arbitrary one." To find the fulfillment
of self through superiority to mere things and without attention to
what others may think about what one does—this is the feat Isabel
supposes Osmond to have accomplished. Actually as she comes tragically to see, Osmond is above all men enslaved by things and by what
he supposes others to be thinking of him. "She had thought it a
grand indifference, an exquisite independence. But indifference was

really the last of his qualities; she had never seen anyone who thought so much of others."

The moral world shared by Isabel and Osmond—a world in which Lord Warburton has no place—is that of the high Emersonian self-culture. In the sordid elegance of Osmond's implacably willed hedonism we discover the final possibilities of corruption in this culture, which is of course no less subject to corruption than any other moral idealism. In Isabel's unhappy career we estimate the tragic implications of an idealism that in effect directs one to seek the rewards of the fully "lived life" without descending from one's high pedestal into its actual conditions. In Isabel's sincere presentation of her essentially spiritual quest as a quest for a real involvement in "the usual chances and dangers" of life lies the tragic irony of the story. And it has, furthermore, the advantage of verisimilitude since that is how an ambitious young woman in the latter part of the nineteenth century—spiritual puritan though she might be—would conceive of her quest, knowing it to be no longer inevitably the part of woman to isolate herself from the world either because of religious conviction or in acquiescence to the conventions about woman's place.

Isabel Archer may be said to have the imagination of romance most notably in the sense that she responds to character intensely only when it conceives of itself at a high level of abstraction and when its acts are symbolic of ideal values. When this imagination is confronted by an appealingly complex human being, such as Lord Warburton, it sees only "a collection of attributes and powers." Like the romancer, Isabel refuses to impute significance to human actions unless they are conceived as being exempt from the ordinary circumstances of life, whereas the genuine novelist sees in ordinary circumstances the inescapable root condition of significant actions.

So, to carry the analogy only one step along, James in the end brings Isabel's point of view around from that of the romancer to that of the novelist. Like *The Blithedale Romance, The Portrait of a Lady* explores the limits of romance. But whereas Hawthorne seems to admit that he cannot be the true novelist and thus surrenders the imagination of the novelist to that of the romancer, James does the opposite, affirming the primacy of the novelist's imagination. But though he rejects romance as a moral view of the world, he assimilates into the very substance of the novel, by means of metaphor and the charm of the heroine herself, the appeal of romance. Thus he is able to meet superabundantly the requirement for the novel which he calls in the Preface to *The American* satisfying "our general sense of the ways things happen" and at the same time he is able to provide the novel with the poetry of romance.

So much, and as it would seem, no more is to be done with *The*

Portrait of a Lady as a romance. In James's books one catches hold of the romance only just as it is disappearing into the thicket of the novel. Thus it is a thankless task to pursue too long and arduously something that is always being assimilated into something else. James is not a romancer like Hawthorne or Melville; he is a novelist to the finger tips.

Drama in *The Portrait of a Lady*

by Richard Poirier

Theatricality is a term which embraces many of the kinds of expression already discussed as characteristic of those people the contact of whose "surface" with the world is limited and preconceived, and who express themselves in accordance with the public expectations which are attached to the rôles they have assumed. It was to have been Isabel's good fortune to escape this fate, even to the extent that James, as her creator, makes a considerable and unusual effort to protect her from being hemmed in by any too exclusive definitions of her character which may be inferred from the dramatic action. His language in the passages of analysis is general to the point of being abstract; he pleads with us not to judge her too readily; he nearly surrenders his own predilection for ambiguity in the interest of rendering her uncomplicated sense of the glamorous; and he so encompasses her with conventionalized personalities that the reader is not apt to criticize in her certain of the characteristics which, in a small way, she shares with them.

The world of Gilbert Osmond may exploit the defects of Isabel's virtues and transform them to the uses of its conventions, but James in his presentation of her will not allow us to "grind her" in the convenient typologies which literary and social convention provide for us. She gives Ralph the impression at Gardencourt that she is a girl who will not act the part which seems to be called for by her situation. An impoverished American girl who, when she first sees Lord Warburton, exclaims, "Oh, I hoped there would be a lord; it's just like a novel!" and who then proceeds to refuse his proposal of marriage, offers such a prospect of original accomplishment that bored and worldly Ralph Touchett is able to believe that here at last is something worth staying alive to witness. It is like a wholly new and different sort of drama which he has never before seen performed. When he convinces his father to leave her a fortune, the old man

"*Drama in* The Portrait of a Lady." *From* The Comic Sense of Henry James *by Richard Poirier (New York: Oxford University Press, 1960; London: Chatto & Windus, Ltd., 1960), pp. 237–46. Copyright © 1960 by Richard Poirier. Reprinted by permission of the publishers.*

remarks that "you speak as if it were for your entertainment," to which Ralph responds, "So it is, a good deal."

Reduced as Ralph is to "mere spectatorship at the game of life," he literally dies when, having lost the freedom with which he tried to endow her, Isabel ceases to be capable of "entertaining" him. On his first visit to Rome after her marriage, he reacts in terms which suggest how even at this point, after only two years with Osmond, she has begun to play the part which her husband requires of her. Instead of the free-spirited, individual self-expression which Ralph had hoped to foster, he finds, partly because she will not admit to him how miserable she is, that

> if she wore a mask, it completely covered her face. There was something fixed and mechanical in the serenity painted upon it; this was not an expression, Ralph said—it was a representation. . . . Her light step drew a mass of drapery behind her; her intelligent head sustained a majesty of ornament. The free, keen girl had become quite another person; what he saw was a fine lady who was supposed to represent something.

The vocabulary is familiar enough—the images which make it sound as though she were engaged in a stage performance, the words "fixed" and "free," and the distinction made between "expression" and "representation." Everywhere in the early fiction, providing indeed the foundation for this study of James, there is evidence of a profoundly felt concern about the distinction between those characters who "express" themselves, and are within range only of James's gentlest irony, and those who "represent" something and whose expression is, therefore, theatrical and conventionalized to the point of self-parody. The progress of the action in *The Portrait of a Lady* is in the direction of making Isabel into such a representative or "fixed" character. There is some justice, therefore, in Isabel's remark to Henrietta that her career has become a comedy:

> "I want to be alone," said Isabel.
> "You won't be that so long as you have got so much company at home."
> "Ah, they are part of the comedy. You others are spectators."
> "Do you call it a comedy, Isabel Archer?" Henrietta inquired severely.
> "The tragedy, then, if you like. You are all looking at me; it makes me uncomfortable."

This exchange occurs just before Henrietta is to escort Ralph back to Gardencourt. Despite his dismay at the changes in Isabel during his first visit, he has returned because, as James tells us:

> What kept Ralph alive was simply the fact that he had not yet seen enough of his cousin; he was not yet satisfied. There was more to come; he wouldn't make up his mind to lose that. He wished to see what she would make of her husband—or what he would make of her. [The

earlier visit] was only the first act of the drama, and he was determined to sit out the performance.

The second "act," eighteen months later, ends with Isabel's request to be left alone and without "spectators." The drama of freedom has become the tragi-comedy of her having "suddenly found the infinite vista of a multiplied life to be a dark, narrow alley, with a dead wall at the end." Her intuition that she is confronting a kind of deadness at the conclusion of some hopeful and confident movement is mirrored in Ralph's acceptance of the fact that, with so little left to appreciate in the drama of Isabel, he has no future prospect except death: "The end of everything was at hand; it seemed to him that he could stretch out his hand and touch the goal." "Everything" for Ralph not only includes Isabel but essentially *is* Isabel.

The implications of this need to be fully recognized, and they provide an astounding illustration of how the drama in the action of James's novels is an imitation of the drama of artistic creativity which goes into them. Ralph's death is to be taken as a metaphor for the fact that Isabel's freedom can no longer be imagined. It can no longer sustain the life of the imagination. She cannot provide for Ralph what Minny Temple, by actually dying, gave James: "The positive relief," as he writes to William, "in thinking of her being removed from her own heroic treatment and placed in kinder hands."

Isabel remains in the hands of Gilbert Osmond. Despite Ralph's last advice ("You must stay here"), and Caspar Goodwood's warning, to which he says Ralph has subscribed ("It will cost you your life!"), Isabel returns to "the house of darkness, the house of dumbness, the house of suffocation." James's adoration, and it can be called that, for superconsciousness leads him at the end of *The Portrait of a Lady* to treat death in a curious way, as a preferable alternative to the deadness which encroaches upon life. There are similar expressions of this, all of them more direct, in his beautifully elegiac passages about the death of Minny Temple in *Notes of a Son and Brother,* in the letters to his mother and to William about Minny, to Grace Norton, after the death of his parents, and in the letter to Howells where, comforting him about the death of his daughter, he is brought to the admission that "I can't talk of death without seeming to say too much—I think so kindly of it as compared with life—the only thing one can compare it to." Life finally denies Isabel the "freedom and rest," to use James's words when he refers to Minny Temple's death, the "eternal freedom" which is given to Minny and to Ralph. With Ralph's death, Isabel ceases to live in the imagination of freedom, and he dies because her life no longer allows him to imagine the possibility that freedom and the life of the world are compatible. The end of the novel reverses the relationship between Isabel and Ralph. It is now she who carries his image in her mind, just as James carried the image of the dead Minny, "as a sort of measure and standard," he wrote William, "of brightness and repose."

The movement towards the end of the novel puts into juxtaposition the varieties of death and deadness which concerned James so deeply and all of those aspects of life which are tainted and deadened by the predictable, the conventional, the merely representative rather than the expressive. All the characters are at last *known* to us in some final way, as if they have become "portraits" indeed, along the order of Browning's Duchess, rather than remained imaginatively alive and changing. Osmond is last seen making a drawing of an antique coin and spouting clichés about "the honour of a thing"; Madame Merle, totally isolated and defeated, decides that she is going to America, and thereby steps out of any associations in which we could continue to conceive of her; Henrietta and Mr. Bantling announce their engagement, as in the sentimental conclusion of a farce, making Isabel conclude that even they are now "conventional." When they tell her their plans, she feels, oddly, as if "the dreariness of the world took on a deeper tinge." Mrs. Touchett, as undeviating and predictable as ever in her attitudes and responses, is even more deadened for us at the conclusion by Isabel's perception that the ageing and lonely woman "saw herself in the future as an old woman without memories." Warburton seems an exception to the general drift of the characters towards colorless inertia. He is at least to be married, though to a girl whose name is never even mentioned. The news makes Isabel feel "as if she had heard of Lord Warburton's death."

Effectively, this leaves Pansy and Caspar as characters who might have a future that allows for expectation, and who could, if this were true, give us reason to imagine them rather than simply to "know" them. But Caspar will, it is clear, continue in his by now stupefying hope of possessing Isabel, and Pansy, as we last saw her at the convent, had "seen the reality. . . . She bowed her pretty head to authority, and only asked of authority to be merciful." While Isabel may promise to return to her, she does so without expectation of doing her much good. Pansy cannot be liberated from Osmond.

The world of possible freedom is, then, discouragingly left to Isabel, who sometimes on the trip "envied Ralph his dying," and Ralph, who is dying in fact. Ironically, it is Caspar Goodwood, of all Isabel's suitors the one who gives the most distinct impression of narrowness of interest and feeling, who makes the final plea for freedom to Isabel: "We can do absolutely as we please." Isabel's reaction to his passionate declaration of love testifies eloquently to the implication that the longing for freedom ultimately becomes, the world being what it is, the desire for death, for the "freedom and rest" which James envied in Minny

Temple. To let Caspar take her in his arms would be, Isabel believes in her momentary desire to let him help her, "the next best thing to dying."

Nothing in James is more movingly rendered, more calculated to extend and exalt our deepest emotions of pity than the scene in which Ralph Touchett dies in Isabel's arms. At last, and for the only time in the novel, two people speak to one another without a semblance of theatricality or shame or self-elevation. This is possible because neither one of them really feels, nor do we, that there is any promise of beauty left past the boundaries of this moment, either in the novel or in the life projected beyond it. Everything that matters to either of them has been done and done badly, but it is only now that Isabel can cry in front of Ralph and can tell herself as well as him: "Oh, Ralph, you have been everything!" Here and only here, at the moment of un-defensive anguish and the recognition of the futility and wastefulness of her life, Isabel finally achieves that absolute union of outward expression and inward feeling for which she has labored. In neither their language nor in James's is there a touch of contrived insincerity or theatricality. Ralph, in particular, speaks with that endearing and direct kindness which, through all the various posturing among the other characters, he has consistently maintained:

> "You won't lose me—you will keep me. Keep me in your heart; I shall be nearer to you than I have ever been. Dear Isabel, life is better; for in life there is love. Death is good—but there is no love."

His promise to be nearer her after his death and his assurance that she will grow young again and will not suffer too much are the final flickerings of his imagination, its last efforts to endow Isabel with some life beyond the point in it which she has reached and beyond, for that matter, the conclusions of the novel. But short of believing in spirits, our imagination cannot, in this matter, subscribe to Ralph's, nor does James expect that it should. Ralph's encouragement of Isabel is an indication of the pathos which James himself experiences when, having created a heroine about whom we are asked to be "more purely ex-pectant" than we would be if she were an ordinary girl, he must see her reduced at last to telling Ralph, the man in the novel who has had for her the greatest expectations: "I should like to stay, as long as seems right."

What has happened to Isabel? And why is it that Ralph's reassuring words tend to be less a prediction of her future than another example of his wonderful capacity, even as he dies, for hope, for loving comfort, even as he is himself most in need of it? These questions are really one question, in the sense that they are sufficiently answered by understanding the significance of Isabel's return to Osmond. Her reasons have been a source of repeated speculation and argument among readers of the novel, largely because the kind of answer usually being sought is not the kind the novel offers to give. For in talking about her return we should be talking about a novel, not about a person, about the relation of her act to James's whole intention, more than about its revelation of her individual psychology. Consider, for example, the supposition that Caspar's kiss in the garden is what impels her to leave for Rome almost immediately. The suggestions of sexual fear in her reactions to Caspar begin very early, they are too recurrent to be ignored, and they reach a melodramatic climax at Gardencourt when he makes his final appeal for her love. Before their meeting, she is anxious to have an excuse for remaining awhile in England, and it is made apparent that her promise to Pansy is not a motive sufficient to make her return to Rome. After his kiss—it was "like a flash of lightning"—and her reflection that she had never really been loved before, she darts away from him, and we are told that "she had not known where to turn; but she knew now. There was a very straight path." It takes her back to the husband whom she has heard Ralph describe as a "sterile dilettante."

We have here another case where particular psychological suggestiveness is more inviting than the expressive rhythm of the whole novel allows us to admit. If Isabel is motivated by sexual fear in this scene, then all her previous acts of high principle might equally be explained, since Caspar figures in all of them, as evasions of psychological distress. From this point of view, the search for freedom becomes in reality the rationalization of an attempt to escape from those personal susceptibilities which, in fact, she is disappointed to find in Henrietta and Mr. Bantling. Henrietta has become subject to "common passions," and her relationship with Mr. Bantling "had not been completely original." It need not be argued that such a reaction to marriage is extremely odd. Just how "original" can a human being afford to be? Admittedly, a case can be made for discussing the novel in terms of the psychological peculiarity of Isabel's conduct. In doing so a wholly new dimension is given to her idealism. It remains commendable, but it submits to consideration as an unconscious theoretical stratagem for avoiding life even as it illustrates its noble possibilities. If we pushed the matter a bit further we would find the psychological basis for the attractiveness which Isabel finds in death and, if still further, the reason why James himself talks about death in his letters as if it offered the promise of freedom which the experience of life denies.

I have already indicated why, on the basis of James's treatment of Isabel throughout the novel, we are not requested to make intense psychological probings into the heroine. No novel can be read as it ought to be except on the principle that when we discover something covert it does not mean that we then give up or transform all that is obvious. Two things seem to me obvious about *The Portrait of a Lady*: first, that it reveals much more about Isabel and about James himself than the author ever intended or expected, and, second, that his actual intention is strongly enough felt over the full course of the narrative so that to put primary emphasis on its unintentional implications is simply to pretend that the experience which the novel offers as a whole is different from what it is. This is a novel of ideas more than of psychology, an imitation of moral action more than a drama of motive. Some may feel, as I do, that *The Portrait of a Lady* would be a greater accomplishment if some of its psychological implications were made a firmer part of the whole design.

James had a very tenuous and unorganized sense of the connection between sexual psychology, on the one hand, and, on the other, the desire for freedom and death. He had a very clear and conscious idea, however, about the relationship between freedom and death, and it is that which comes through to us from the final chapters. What Caspar offers her in the garden is an old call to action and freedom: "The world is all before us." While the intensity of her reaction to Caspar deserves the closest attention, the reasons for her refusal to go away with him need no explanation. She is simply not deeply enough in love with him nor has she ever been. When she hurries away from him, however, she is also escaping his call to leave the "garden" of her dreams now that, like Eden after the fall, it has become a place of desolation. The Miltonic echo in his plea is unmistakably placed there. The same line occurs much earlier in the novel when Isabel sees her relatives off for America. Having done her duty by these figures out of her past, and in possession of what seems unhampered independence, she walks away from the station into the London fog: "The world lay all before her— she could do whatever she chose." In James's use of the phraseology of *Paradise Lost* ("The world lay all before them, where to choose/Their place of rest . . . "), there is not only a Miltonic sadness, but also an irony derived from the fact that neither Isabel nor Caspar is free to choose anything. His life is in useless bondage to his love for her, while hers is dedicated to its errors. And there is nothing in her act which holds the promise, as does Adam and Eve's, of eventual happiness through suffering, even though Ralph assures her that there is. Her action is absolutely within the logic of her Emersonian idealism, so much so that the logic takes its vengeance. In effect she tells the reader, to borrow from "The Transcendentalist," that "you think me the child of my circumstances: I make my circumstance,"—including, one might add, "my own misery." It is of no importance to her that, in fact, she has been so calculatingly deceived by other people that it is preposterous to assume all the responsibility for her own past. To admit this

would be finally to subscribe to Madame Merle's view that the "self"
is determined, in part, by "an envelope of circumstances" that one does
not always create. Isabel's action at the end is fully consistent with
everything she does earlier. Now, however, she asserts her idealism of
self not in innocence but in full knowledge of the world. For that
reason, freedom, which was the condition of self-creation, becomes a
form of indifference to the fact that returning to Rome will, as Caspar
admonishes, cost her her life.

Some Rooms From
"The Houses that James Built"

by R. W. Stallman

In his Preface to *The Portrait of a Lady* Henry James discusses his
novel as though it were a stately edifice—"It came to be a square and
spacious house"—with nothing out of line, scale or perspective in his
construction of it. Caspar Goodwood, as we have seen, is rendered as
a belfry tower; Isabel, in Ralph's metaphoric view of her, figures as a
house: "He surveyed the edifice from the outside and admired it
greatly; he looked in at the windows and received an impression of
proportions equally fair." This appraisal applies not only to Isabel,
but also to *The Portrait of a Lady*. What follows applies not only to
Ralph's relationship to Isabel, but also to the reader's relationship to
her; she bewilders us, too: "But he felt that he saw it only by glimpses
and that he had not yet stood under the roof." For Ralph "The door
was fastened, and though he had keys in his pocket he had a conviction
that none of them would fit." Henry James defines the art of fiction as
"the house of fiction" and, in retracing his process of composition, he
speaks of the artist as though he were the architect and builder of a
literary edifice. His own magnificent structure was begun with a single
corner-stone—"the conception of a certain young woman affronting
her destiny"—and erected brick by brick until the finished whole
measured up to the blueprint. After submitting the first three installments for serial publication in *Macmillan's Magazine* (1880), he pro-
ceeded to complete the novel *during* its serial publication; what
remained to complete the whole permitted no deviations from what
had already seen print. He tempted fate and nursed his luck; mind
you, no revisions! Considering the hazard, one marvels quite as much
at *how* he brought *The Portrait of a Lady* to perfection as *at the*

"Some Rooms from 'The Houses that James Built'" by R. W. Stallman. From
Texas Quarterly, *I (Winter, 1958), 181–84, 189–92. The essay appears in a revised
and expanded version in* The Houses that James Built *by R. W. Stallman (East
Lansing: Michigan State University Press, 1961). Copyright © 1961 by Michigan
State University Press. Reprinted by permission of* Texas Quarterly *and Michigan
State University Press.*

achieved masterpiece itself. Second to *Moby Dick, The Portrait of a Lady* strikes me as the richest perfection in American literature.

Like the Pyncheon house in Hawthorne's *House of the Seven Gables,* the houses in *A Portrait of a Lady* serve to interpret their inhabitants metaphorically. As artist, James was addicted to the symbolic significance of *things:* a cracked tea-cup, a golden bowl, works of sculpture or painting or music, tapestries, ancient coins. By such minute particulars James renders symbolically the nature and plight of his fictional characters—in *The Portrait of a Lady* notably by the metaphors of gardens and houses. Technically, the gap between James's first and second novel is immense, and it is James's study of Hawthorne that accounts for the difference. James, as every student of Hawthorne recognizes, refined upon Hawthorne's symbolic devices. Midway through *Roderick Hudson* (1874, published 1876) James deposited his hero in the Villa Pandolfini. It is the same villa that Gilbert Osmond inhabits in *The Portrait* (1881), in point of fact, the Villa Mercedes on the Piazza Bellosguardo. James visited here in 1869 (cf. *Letters,* I, 23). From the formal gardens of the Villa Mercedes can be seen "the crenelated tower of a neighboring villa," as James mentions in *Roderick Hudson.* This is Villa Montauto, where Hawthorne once lived. It figures as the crenelated tower that Kenyon visits in Chapter XXIV of *The Marble Faun.* James was especially fond of Hawthorne's Roman allegory, but *Roderick Hudson* is proof enough that at the time of its composition he had not yet read *The Marble Faun.* He had read it, however, by the time he wrote his second novel, *The American* (1877). Here he employs the same symbolic devices as in *The Portrait,* whereas his first novel is devoid of symbolism.

The Villa Mercedes (then known as the Villa Castellani) has a lovely *cortile,* reputed to be among the best preserved in Florence, with an ancient well and a private chapel. In *Roderick Hudson* it is described as "a great cool *cortile,* graced round about with light arches and heavily-corniced doors of majestic altitude and furnished on one side with a grand old archaic well." *The Portrait,* employing Hawthorne's chiaroscuro style, presents it as a "high court, where a clear shadow rested below and a pair of light-arched galleries, facing each other above, caught the upper sunshine upon their slim columns and the flowering plants in which they were dressed." It is here that Isabel first visits Osmond, and the setting as rendered with its shadow-sunlight attributes is therefore appropriate symbolically. Roderick Hudson's villa, on the contrary, has no metaphoric import; it is simply a villa— that and nothing more. In *Roderick Hudson* the ample front of the villa ("pierced with windows of various sizes, no one of which, save those on the ground floor, was of the same level as the other"), and the *cortile,* and the rare elevation and great view from the hilltop *piazzetta* sloping straight up from the Porta Romana—all these things remain unused, symbolically, and merely picturesque. Mary Garland feels merely "the sovereign charm of the place. . . . She fell in love on the spot with Florence, and used to look down wistfully at the towered city from their terraced garden." In *The Portrait* nothing is merely picturesque. Here realism is extended into symbolism by metaphors of designed purpose.

Dark houses metaphorically rendered Isabel's history. Disillusioned after her marriage to Osmond, she regards her marriage as "the house of darkness, the house of dumbness, the house of suffocation. Osmond's beautiful mind gave it neither light nor air; Osmond's beautiful mind indeed seemed to peep down from a small high window and mock at her." It is from Isabel's point of view that Osmond is associated with "a small high window," whereas in fact Osmond presents to the world quite a different front as we know by the metaphoric Palazzo Roccanera in Rome, the house of the Osmonds. Here, as also at Osmond's Florence villa where he courted Isabel, "the proportions of the windows and even the details of the cornice had quite the grand air." Seen by Edward Rosier when he first courts Pansy, Osmond's daughter, the palace seems like a fortress imprisoning his lady-love. It also imprisons Isabel; but it is she herself, rather than Osmond, who has imprisoned Isabel Archer. For the Rome palace duplicates the imprisoning house at Albany where Isabel's history began; it is the Albany house all over again, done on the grand style. Beginning with the Albany house and concluding with the Rome palace, Isabel ends her quest where she began it—in a house of darkness.

As Ned Rosier rescues Pansy from the Palazzo Roccanera at the end of the novel, so at the start Mrs. Daniel Touchett, like the fairy godmother comes to rescue the princess from her dungeon, gives our heroine her freedom from "a kind of domestic fortress." As Mrs. Touchett sees the Albany house, "It's a very bad house"; the parallel is Ned Rosier's view of the Rome palace:

> It seemed to him of evil omen that the young lady he wished to marry, and whose fastidious father he doubted of his ability to conciliate, should be immured in a kind of domestic fortress, a pile which bore a stern old Roman name, which smelt of historic deeds, of crime and craft and violence, which was mentioned in "Murray" and visited by tourists who looked, on a vague survey, disappointed and depressed, and which had frescoes by Caravaggio in the *piano nobile* and a row of mutilated statues and dusty urns in the wide, nobly-arched loggia overhanging the damp court where a fountain gushed out of a mossy niche.

As for the identity of the Palazzo Roccanera, James tells us only that it is "a high house in the very heart of Rome; a dark and massive structure overlooking a sunny *piazzetta* in the neighborhood of the

Farnese Palace." James describes the palace exactly as it is, omitting to
mention only the Cortona frescoes in the library. (The Caravaggio
painting is *Saint Peter and Saint Paul*.) While it is less ostentatious
than either the Palazzo Farnese or the Palazzo Barberini, it is more
impressive architecturally than many other palaces in Rome, including the Palazzo Caetani adjoining it. The Palazzo Antici Mattei is a
stately and somber structure, and furthermore it is picturesque. It is
for these reasons that James selected this palace and not another, because it suited admirably Osmond's character and Isabel's (particularly
her predilection for the picturesque). The palace is in the measure of
Osmond's social ambitions, although Isabel claims that she "and her
husband had chosen this habitation for the love of local colour."
Osmond's motive, however, "was as vulgar as the art was great. To surround his interior with a sort of invidious sanctity, to tantalize society
with a sense of exclusion, to make people believe his house was different from every other, to impart to the face that he presented to the
world a cold originality—this was the ingenious effort of the personage
to whom Isabel had attributed a superior morality."

James drew upon actualities for the germinal seeds of his invented,
consciously schematized, and frequently cryptographic compositions.
The illuminating point is how he fashioned the given situation, person, thing, or house into a designed whole: how he converted the
literal to the symbolic. Without mentioning Osmond, James creates
a sense of his presence while describing the Osmond villa in Florence:
its windows are of "noble proportions, extremely architectural; but
their function seemed less to offer communication with the world than
to defy the world to look in. They were massively crossbarred, and
placed at such a height that curiosity, even on tiptoe, expired
before it reached them." That is exactly the Villa Mercedes, here converted to a metaphor signifying Osmond. The villa's "antique, solid,
weather-worn, yet imposing front had a somewhat incommunicative
character." The villa's front is "pierced with a few windows in irregular relations," suggestive of Osmond's own irregular relations (*i.e.*, with
Madame Merle). Furthermore, the piazza is "of crooked shape." It is
small and "empty."

When Isabel promises to return to the villa another time, she is
cornered by Osmond at "one of the angles of the terrace." Angles,
crooked piazza, and irregular windows—all hint at Osmond's moral
obliquity. Osmond's massive and forbidding villa foretells the domestic fortress of their Rome palace and harks back to the gloomy Albany
house. What James says of Osmond's villa also describes Osmond's
palace: "There was something grave and strong in the place; it looked
somehow as if, once you were in, you would need an act of energy to
get out. For Isabel, however, there was of course as yet no thought of

getting out, but only of advancing." Advancing not at all, she ends in a house that duplicates the houses of her courtship days, namely Osmond's Florence villa and Mrs. Touchett's Palazzo Crescentini. James's characters in *The Portrait* are analogous one to another, and so too are their houses. Book I foretells the heroine's career by the houses James built there. . . .

All the crucial events in our heroine's career occur in houses—not in gardens. When Lord Warburton proposes to her on the sunlit lawns of Gardencourt, what's in her mind is Caspar's courtship as announced in the letter she has just then finished reading; and when years later Caspar comes to rescue her from her husband, what is in her mind is the visit that Lord Warburton had made but a few minutes ago to bid her goodbye. Just as on that former occasion six years ago when Lord Warburton proposed and she had felt frightened, turning "quickly back to the house," so now again when Caspar—to her terror—kisses her, she takes flight back to a dimly-lit house. She finds sanctuary in dark houses. In gardens she defers "the need of really facing her crisis."

She confronts crises in houses because houses represent the accumulated refinement and corruption of civilization, our tragic history echoing throughout the House of Experience. " 'Who are you—what are you?' Isabel murmured. 'What have you to do with my husband?' " It is inside her own house that she discovers the treachery of Madame Merle. Her first intimation of it occurs on her returning to the Palazzo Roccanera after gathering flowers on the Campagna, a scene of Eden-innocence, whereupon she finds her husband in a compromising situation; he is sitting while Madame Merle stands. "Their relative positions, their absorbed mutual gaze, struck her as something detected." Their conspiracy against Isabel is plotted not in a garden, but in a house—in the Countess Gemini's apartment. Here Osmond sits "half-behind, half-beside Madame Merle's chair," by which situation we know that it is Madame Merle who instigates the plot and who dominates Osmond. She instructs him to proceed to Rome in pursuit of the woman she has chosen for him. His courtship continues at Saint Peter's Cathedral and then at the opera house (the pivotal scenes of the book), and next we find Osmond proposing to Isabel in the Hotel de Paris in Rome.

Courtships occur both in gardens and in houses, but the proposals resulting in marriage—Osmond's at the hotel and Ned Rosier's in the yellow room of the Osmond palace—occur in houses. Osmond courts Isabel first at Casa Touchett in Florence, then at his own villa and in its garden, and next at the Palazzo Crescentini again. When she returns from the East she lives for three weeks in Madame Merle's Rome apartment, and here in the house of his former mistress Osmond courts Miss Archer. Whereas it is on the sunny lawns of Gardencourt that

Lord Warburton proposes to her, it is inside the house—in the art gallery—that she discloses her reasons for rejecting him. Here, as in the previous scene in Gardencourt's art gallery, Isabel reveals again her lack of insight—amidst works of art of which she is ignorant.

Our heroine's destiny is plotted between two deaths. They chart her progress from concealed ignorance to revealed truth. When Ralph is on his deathbed, Isabel unmasks: "She had lost all her shame, all wish to hide things." It takes his dying to bring her round to reveal now the truth of her plight, whereas before this crisis Ralph Touchett, as he had surmised, "should learn nothing; for him she would always wear a mask." At the first death in Gardencourt, while old Mr. Touchett is dying, she meets Madame Merle. She is mistaken about Madame Merle at the start: she supposes her a French lady—in that light she seems to Isabel all the more romantic. Like Emma Bovary, Isabel is possessed of the romantic malady. Gardencourt, Lockleigh, the Casa Touchett, even Osmond's Rome palace, as well as his Florence villa and Osmond himself—everything strikes Isabel as romantic. She expresses the same illusion about the second-rate Verdi opera as previously she had attached to her grandmother's ugly house in Albany: everything seems to her picturesque. She is impressed by Madame Merle's piano-playing, but what she fails to notice is that it is indiscreet of Madame Merle to be playing the piano while she is a guest in the house of her dying host. As her sincerity is here impugned, so is Osmond's when he proposes to Isabel at the Hotel de Paris. He proposes in a setting of gaudy decor not appropriate for the declared sincerity of his professed love. Osmond himself recognizes the disparity. His declared sincerity is commented on, as it were, by the mawkishly decorated room of vaulted ceilings "painted over with naked muses and cherubs. For Osmond the place was ugly to distress; the false colours, the sham splendour were like vulgar, bragging, *lying talk*." His declaration of love affects her with the sharp pang that suggests "the slipping of a fine bolt—backward, forward, she couldn't have said. which." The answer is backward; for the slipping of the bolt has to do with the bolted door of the unused and condemned half of the Albany house, to which the bolted door was nevertheless the proper entrance. The bolted door signifies her sexual frigidity (even after her marriage, as we know by her cold yellow bedroom, she remains essentially virginal); it signifies also her propensity for sanctuary from life and the proprieties of protective conventions. "You were not to be trapped by the conventional," Ralph moans; Osmond represents Convention personified: "I'm not in the least stupidly conventional. I'm just the contrary."

"If one's two-sided it's enough," Isabel remarks at Ralph's claim that she is many-sided. Her two sides are represented by the house-garden and the dark-light ambivalence of her double consciousness. Her doubleness is represented by the Albany house—it is a double house. The green paper sidelights at the door beguile Miss Archer with unwary optimism. They suggest the Eve-like innocence of one whose nature has about it the attributes of a "garden-like quality, a suggestion of perfume and murmuring boughs, of shady bowers and lengthening vistas." At the Albany house all of Isabel's visits "had the flavour of peaches." Gardencourt, where "the wide carpet of turf that covered the level hill-top seemed but the extension of a luxurious interior," duplicates the Albany house; for here too nature is at one with the house itself. Gardencourt also has its doubleness. Its true front is not the side facing the river, where life seems in flux; its true front "was quite in another quarter." Both houses deny contact with the outer world. Henrietta Stackpole would like Gardencourt "a great deal better if it were a boarding-house"; the Albany house offers "the appearance of a bustling provincial inn kept by a gentle old landlady who sighed a great deal and never presented a bill. Isabel of course knew nothing about bills; but even as a child she thought her grandmother's home romantic." Gardencourt strikes her as romantic, because she cannot judge houses, but it is rather "a dreadfully dull house." To get impressions of *real* life for the *Interviewer*, Henrietta leaves Gardencourt for London. By their incommunicative fronts the Osmond villa and palace link with the deceptive front of the Albany house. It was said of that side of his villa facing the crooked *piazzetta* and commerce with the Florentine world, "*It was the mask*, not the face of the house."

Like Pansy, Isabel at the Albany house "had no wish to look out, for this would have interfered with her theory that there was a strange, unseen place on the other side—a place which became to the child's imagination, according to its different moods, a region of delight or of terror." Isabel had never opened that bolted door, nor removed that green paper to look into the vulgar street filled with the noisy hum of schoolchildren from the Dutch house opposite her sanctuary. Outside are cosmic treacheries of which Isabel as yet knows nothing, but which overtake her in the end. "A cruel, cold rain fell heavily. . . . Isabel, however, gave as little heed as possible to cosmic treacheries; she kept her eyes on her book and tried to fix her mind." But her mind, like the bolted door, is already fixed. Osmond's proposal disconcerts her because she has a dread of surprises that force her to choose and decide. "I don't like such surprises," she tells Caspar when he appears unannounced at the Hotel Pratt apartment. Ralph, on the contrary, is "extremely fond of the unexpected" and counts upon Isabel's giving grand example of it. The grand example is Caspar Goodwood ("I've no plans.") Mrs. Touchett thinks the Unpredictable can't touch her; that is *her* illusion. "You know that as a general thing I don't expect."

Expectations, great plans, and theories epitomize our heroine, and it is her predilection for fixed ideas that trap her. "Isabel Archer was a young person of many theories; her imagination was remarkably active."

Illusions versus realities, theories and fixed ideas punctured by reality, inform the substance of the novel. While James focuses his theme of Illusions of Appearances versus Reality in his heroine, he exempts none of his personages from the affliction that Isabel suffers from. Even Madame Merle has her illusions, although unlike Isabel she had never had "any illusions of *Intelligence*. She hopes she may marry a great man; that has always been her idea. She has waited and watched and plotted and prayed; but she has never succeeded. I don't call Madame Merle a success, you know," says the Countess Gemini. ". . . Her great idea has been to be the incarnation of propriety. She has always worshipped that god. There should be no scandal about Caesar's wife, you know; and, as I say, she has always hoped to marry Caesar." Osmond is no Caesar; that is one reason she would not marry him. Accomplished in the fine arts, as well as in the fine art of manipulating her friends, Madame Merle replaces Henrietta Stackpole as Isabel's ideal. She rejects the artless Henrietta (Caspar and Lord Warburton are in the same category) for the artful Madame Merle, who acts "as if the art of life were some clever trick she had guessed." Although later, when it is then too late, she loses "the desire to know this lady's clever trick," at the start she "would have given anything for lessons in this art." Seemingly "imperturbable, inscrutable, impenetrable," Miss Archer conceals because, like the moon, she has no light of her own to offer. "You conceal everything; I haven't really come near you," Caspar complains. Though she seems to her friends unpredictable, both in her rejection of Lord Warburton and in her engagement to Osmond, Isabel is as predictable as the moon itself. We know her various phases from the start; one phase is her quest for enlightenment, another is her quest for darkness.

Nostalgic Poison

by Maxwell Geismar

Rather like *The American,* the opening of [*The Portrait of a Lady*] was that of leisurely, old-fashioned social comedy; the tone was warm, genial, entertaining. Again there were the overtones of great wealth, high culture, and "old world" sensitivity in the exchange of pleasantries between Lord Warburton and the Touchetts, and when the charming young American girl first encounters the vista of the lawn, the great trees, the silvery Thames, the old house, the British dogs. In one sense *The Portrait of a Lady* was an engaging domestic drama of the international scene; on this level it summarized and capped all of the early James's romantic visions of "the dream of Europe." We first see the eccentric Mrs. Touchett, who has brought Isabel Archer to England, when she is completely dressed for dinner and embracing her son with her gloved hands.

If the mother image in *Washington Square* was that of a beautiful and dead woman, the psychological cause of her daughter's ruin, the Mrs. Touchett of the *Portrait* is also separated, by her choice of an Italian residence, from her British-American family. Isabel herself, with her innocence and cleverness, her "irregular education," her strong will and high temper; her determination to learn about life and not to be bored, is a superior evocation of the series of young American girls who are the products of wealth and the victims of Europe. Is she a limited medium of literary consciousness, a rather thin and cool and "intellectual" figure as a heroine and a woman? But this whole line of early Jamesian heroines, these young American girls who were in reality rich, spoiled, untutored products of the new American fortunes, were romanticized and idealized by a writer whose own charm of craft carried along these rather dubious vehicles. Similarly Lord Warburton is a curious type of nobleman of the newest pattern, "a reformer, a radical, a contemner of ancient ways." He has a hundred thousand (pounds) a year, and owns fifty thousand acres. He has half

a dozen houses to live in, a seat in Parliament, elegant taste in literature, art, science, and in charming young ladies. But "the victim of a
critical age," he is James's concept of a royal revolutionist.

"I should delight in seeing a revolution," says Isabel Archer herself.
But in such a case, she adds, "I think I should be a high, proud loyalist.
One sympathizes more with them, and they've a chance to behave so
exquisitely. I mean so picturesquely." Yes, the England of the 1870's
was in the throes of a social crisis produced by the injustices of the in-
dustrial revolution. But again the early James notion of "history," very
much like his heroine's, was concerned not so much with principles as
with the pictorial. "If I were he," says Isabel to the nobleman's two
sisters, the Misses Molyneux, "I should wish to fight to the death: I
mean for the heritage of the past . . . I should hold it tight." Yet
Warburton was acceptable to James as an upper-class radical, at least,
or as the symbol of one rather than the fact. The only valid social criticism, or social commentary, in *The Portrait of a Lady* is in the portrait of Henrietta Stackpole, the brassy American lady journalist who
snoops around the British aristocracy for the benefit of the democratic
"free press." She is an amusing caricature at times; she does indeed
"smell of the Future—it almost knocks one down!" as James said. But
Howells, before James, and Edith Wharton after him were equally
sharp on the yellow journalism of the period.

The sensitive and sick Ralph Touchett is the familiar Jamesian ob-
server in the novel. The spiritual guardian of Isabel, and then her material benefactor, he is really the other half, the conscious half of Isabel, or of a central protagonist in the *Portrait* which is feminine in
essence. (Ralph's family name is a cross between "touching," which he
is, and one who hardly dares to touch; while the large share of the
family fortune which he gives to Isabel as a token of his affection is
in the best vein of Jamesian romance about the world of the inheri-
tors.) James had actually divided up his own sensibilities between these
two central figures, as in *Roderick Hudson*; while the arrival of Caspar
Goodwood in the novel points up the emotional deficiency in Lord
Warburton himself. "She liked him too much to marry him, that was
the truth," Isabel reflects about the British lord, but he was indeed a
personage. "She had never yet known a personage; there had been no
personages . . . in her life; there were probably none at all in her
native land."

Thus *The Portrait of a Lady* was a compendium of early James prejudices, and Caspar himself is a rude, aggressive symbol of "New World
vitality." But there are other elements here—his mere arrival "made
the air sultry" around Isabel, and she is terrified of him, as she admits.
"There was a disagreeably strong push, a kind of hardness of presence,
in his way of rising before her . . . Caspar Goodwood expressed for

her an energy—and she had already felt it as a power—that was of his very nature." He is the only symbol of biological or sexual energy in the novel; this post-Civil War American industrialist is a kind of early D. H. Lawrence character. "But it was as if something large and confused, something dark and ugly, would have to call upon him: he was not after all in harmony with mere smug peace and greed and gain . . ." And Isabel, drawn to him physically, has to get rid of him. "Yes, you don't at all delight me, you don't fit in, not in any way, just now." "One would think you were going to commit some atrocity!" says Caspar in return, directly before the entrance of Mme. Merle. And he is right. This is an effective climax in the early part of the *Portrait*; even though one notices that James has divided off the qualities of love, for Isabel, between two equally impossible suitors.

Mme. Merle is the old-world magician, as her name indicates, whom Isabel has been asking to initiate her into the "mystery of life," and who leads her into her fatal entrapment. Here again James used a "false," or at least a highly melodramatic plot to carry forward the action in the last half of the novel; and yet, on such an improbable base, the last half is perhaps the best part of the novel. What is remarkable is the virtuosity of James's craft which could carry forward such a thin, pure heroine—empty of all real knowledge or real experience—and such a limited view of life, based on such peculiar propositions, even to this point. It is Mme. Merle who sets Gilbert Osmond after Isabel's fortune for the sake of little Pansy, the child of a previous affair between these two former lovers. (These two lovers, who know each other so well, have no love left, apparently; no affection, no memories, except a cold understanding of material gain.) Yes, melodrama, plus an Italian travelogue, constitute the real medium of the second half of *The Portrait of a Lady*, which is also in a sense a completely different, or a second novel.

Osmond himself, with his old curtains and crucifixes; with his bibelots, his pictures, his medallions and tapestries, and his dependence on "beauty" as the secret of existence, is the portrait of a pure esthete; a "collector." "He had consulted his taste in everything—his taste alone, perhaps, as a sick man consciously incurable consults at last only his lawyer," James wrote, and he was projecting another facet of his own temperament. "I had no prospects, I was poor . . . I had no talents even; I was simply the most fastidious young gentleman living," Osmond tells Isabel. Yet he and Mme. Merle liven up this cold-blooded and unbelievable plot to entrap the American heiress; these two, and the "Fayaway" young Pansy, and the Countess Gemini herself. This highly compromised character, as James said, by no means a blank sheet, but one that had been written over "in a variety of hands," and who exhibited "the mere floating fragments of a wrecked renown," is another message of warning to poor blind Isabel.

What Isabel is seeking from Osmond is the life of experience; what she gets from their marriage is the cold life of cultivation. This mistress of rejection arrives only at an apex of renunciation. And now James piles twist on twist of narrative complication to sustain the climax of *The Portrait of a Lady*. Ralph is slowly dying, just living long enough, as he says, for his "curiosity" to glean the conclusion of Isabel's tragic marriage—an odd motive for survival. Lord Warburton, now the "famous radical" of the London *Times* at least, re-enters Isabel's life as a potential suitor for Pansy's hand, this foster-daughter of the foster-mother whom he still loves. How fond James is of these deliberately contrived and ambiguous human relations! Notice the ingenious "domestic" and love relationships that prevail at large in the novel. Pansy's true mother, Mme. Merle, marries off her former lover for the sake of her daughter. Isabel's own child dies shortly after her marriage, while she devotes herself to Osmond's (and Mme. Merle's) child, whom the father scorns. Warburton returns as the father-lover of Pansy, while he still desires the lost wife-mother figure of Isabel. The touching relation of Isabel and Ralph becomes that of brother and sister, but of an "adopted" brother who also confers on Isabel the fortune which is meant to bring her happiness and leads to her ruin.

Was this a curious kind of oedipal fantasy, or mere fictional ingenuity, or something else still? That is the question to be determined. It is a central issue in James's craft, in his real view of life: a causative agent as well as a literary curiosity, compounded of incest and ambiguity. Meanwhile Isabel, symbol of Puritan conscience, is determined to atone for her own errors of judgment. "It was impossible to pretend that she had not acted with her eyes open; if ever a girl was a free agent she had been. A girl in love was doubtless not a free agent; but the sole source of her mistake had been within herself. There had been no plot, no snare; she had looked and considered and chosen. When a woman had made such a mistake, there was only one way to repair it—just immensely (oh, with the highest grandeur!) to accept it . . ." But this "grandeur" of the Jamesian heroine, and this lofty, touching moral suffering and resignation, were also highly suspect— were theatrical, and based on an altogether false foundation. In fact, there *was* a plot and a snare (James's own plot and snare); and it was Isabel's pride and her vanity, and perhaps her fear of life, which prevailed over her common sense, and her capacity for experience.

The later portrait of Isabel Archer contained some of James's most effective and famous descriptions of the life of restriction, depression, failure. "It was the house of darkness, the house of dumbness, the house of suffocation." These were the emotions that James knew best; and which paralleled some of his personal passages of anxiety and renunciation in the *Notebooks*. But there also was a final paradox in his famous early heroine and his own view of life. When Isabel Archer realizes the depths of her own degradation—and the absolutely contrived situation which has led her there—why shouldn't she pick up and go? Or rather, pick up her fortune and go? It is bad enough to be trapped by life; but it is totally inexcusable—isn't it?—to remain trapped by altogether contrived circumstances in life. Isabel's relation with Pansy is never convincing, while the child herself is a dubious symbol of the European jeune fille. Isabel's power over Mme. Merle, in the end, is sufficient to send that sorceress into exile in America; the worst of all possible Jamesian fates. Just as the plot of the *Portrait* is never quite credible, except as entertainment, the resolution of the novel is strained to fit the Jamesian moral rather than the realities of the European existence he was describing. The human truth of the story is constrained, or contorted on the Procrustean frame of both the author's initial concept and his limited sense of experience—or of the lack of alternatives in human choice.*

The *Portrait* was in this sense a Victorian "novel of complications" raised to a new height of moral or intellectual analysis. It used an early and quite orderly "stream of consciousness"; but never the true currents of the unconscious; which yet, in a curious way, James somehow suggested. He could be far more free sexually, about the disreputable Italian Countess Gemini—"with her trunks, her dresses, her chatter, her falsehoods, her frivolity, the strange, the unholy legend of the number of her lovers." Nevertheless, all of his *heroine's* relations, perhaps her marriage itself, must remain pure, lofty, exalted, and, in the end, self-sacrificial, renunciatory, chaste. There is another interesting scene where Caspar Goodwood is almost overcome by his passion for Isabel—

> Now that he was alone with her all the passion he had never stifled surged into his senses; it hummed in his eyes and made things swim round him. The bright, empty room grew dim and blurred, and through the heaving veil he felt her hover before him with gleaming eyes and parted lips.

But if Caspar's seizure is almost feminine in essence, Isabel, frightened of what she reads in his face, preserves her forced smile and her composure. " 'I suppose you wish to bid me good-bye?' she said."

* But compare Robert W. Stallman (*The Houses that James Built*, 1961), one of the most recent and fervent converts to the New Criticism, who declares that —"Second to *Moby Dick*, *The Portrait of a Lady* strikes me as the richest perfection in American literature." Well, I've already suggested that Isabel Archer would make a strange mate for the demonic, rebellious Ahab; and what poles, what worlds apart these two novels are in fact. How can recent American criticism lose all sense of values, of distinctions, of judgment in this infatuated, absurd fashion?

There is still the embrace he forces upon her, which confirms all her distaste for him. "His kiss was like white lightning, a flash that spread, and spread again, and stayed; and it was extraordinarily as if, while she took it, she felt each thing in his hard manhood that had least pleased her, each aggressive fact of his face, his figure, his presence, justified of its intense identity and made one with this act of possession. So had she heard of those wrecked and under water following a train of images before they sank. But when darkness returned she was free." Free indeed: to continue her solitary existence of suffering, the pursuit of her own heightened sensibility at the expense of all common human pleasure, companionship, fulfillment in human relations. In this sense the ending of the novel was never ambiguous. The first major heroine of James's was a woman who teased, flirted with and then fled from all of her possible lovers; while she took the one man who would never awaken her, and who had to destroy her.

This was the meaning of *The Portrait of a Lady* in any kind of depth interpretation, and perhaps it is still the reason why, despite the inadequacy of the story's origins and conclusions—and of its professed and "conscious" moral—the novel still attracts, even while it may puzzle us. Was the early James even dimly aware of the true nature of this heroine whom he described with such charm and grace and then with such magniloquence of moral grandeur? But this was a writer, as we shall see, whose unconscious emotions continued to project a series of figures, situations, and relations which are often directly opposed to, in flat contradiction to, the conscious purposes of his craft. This great "analyst" of modern American fiction, and of modern criticism, was aware of everything except his own inner springs of creative action.

The skill of craft, apparent even as early as this novel, was designed to compensate for, even to conceal, the inadequate fictional concepts of James's—to bridge the gap between his dubious propositions and his foreshortened conclusions. On the conscious level *The Portrait of a Lady* must be viewed only as a kind of superior romance melodrama which is entertaining to read, and completely inadequate as serious literary commentary on the life of James's period, or certainly our own. That the novel has another hidden source of interest is due simply to the unacknowledged conflict between the intuitions of the artist, including his own sexual fears, inhibitions, and aversions which are projected through his revealing heroine, and the "literary intention" which he consciously rendered to his readers and, yes, to himself.

News of Life

by Quentin Anderson

James's use of "portrait" in his title has a double significance. His "lady" makes the mistake which mankind generally makes. She tries to make the world reflect her, instead of perceiving that it reflects the sources of being. At the end of the novel Isabel sets about correcting this error, as we all must. But Osmond's appropriation of Isabel *as* a portrait is an ultimate sin; he tries to make the young American girl, representative of the promise of life, reflect him. He appropriates what might become his conscience. This is not marriage, but concubinage. Isabel's greed is worldly, and corrigible; Osmond's is spiritual, and it damns him. . . . Osmond (whose name suggests something fixed and dead, bony or of the earth) stands at one of the limits of moral motion. When Isabel comes to fear herself, her fear will be of what he represents, absolute or spiritual greed. Having declared at the outset, "I only want to see for myself," she sees Osmond as an image which answers *her* sense of *her* claims on the world. She marries the man who *thinks* he is the first gentleman in Europe. In this way she creates the "blasted circle" round which she walks, and comes to the realization classic among James's central characters: "I'm afraid," she tells Ralph during their last meeting in Rome, "Afraid of myself." While she has become afraid, Osmond has become ever more exigent; he holds her on a tighter and tighter rein, since he needs her to reflect him. His prime desire is to "preserve appearances."

This phrase has for James a weight, a force, which is hard to exaggerate. Those who try to "preserve appearances" at such a cost are trying to preserve false institutional forms which are in deadly opposition to moral spontaneity and the forms to which it gives rise. They represent what the elder James called the "church," an organized inversion of love and truth. Isabel's return to Rome, the house of life in which she has encountered her other self, is emblematically consistent, although it may seem to the reader of the novel to depend too much on

"News of Life." From The American Henry James *by Quentin Anderson (New Brunswick, N. J.: Rutgers University Press, 1957), pp. 187–92. Copyright © 1957 by Rutgers, The State University. Reprinted by permission of the publisher.*

an exaggerated idea of the sanctity of marriage, or an exaggerated estimate of Isabel's ability to help Pansy Osmond, who, as the novel presents her, is in a hopeless position.

The novel closes at the moment when Isabel has her foot on the
threshold of the adult world. She knows what Maisie knows at the end
of the novel in which she figures. She recognizes that one must fear
one's own impulses. And something more: All the aesthetic values, all
the "old things," the whole burden of the human past which she and
Osmond have collaborated in seizing, have now to be reseen, not as
possessions, but as evidence of the divine and devilish, of the mixed
character of man. She is in the state of the American setting foot in
Europe only to exclaim: "Look what I have gone and done!"

Ending the novel here, James leaves on the reader's hands the question of what ultimately happens to Isabel. When she goes back to
Pansy, she does not go back to the possibility of action. Pansy is and
will remain a hopeless sacrifice to Osmond's respect for "appearances."
It is best that she become a nun, for the only alternative is that she be
appropriated. Even the elder James is ready to recognize the function
of nunneries in Europe. They may save subject women from appropriation.

Since Pansy cannot be helped by Isabel, Isabel's return is a return to
the struggle with herself, to the contention with that group of impulses
in her of which Osmond is the ultimate expression. James has sub-
stituted an emblematic conclusion for a dramatic one. His notebooks
suggest that he found this satisfactory, but the book clearly seems more
rounded off to him than it can to the uninitiated reader.

The clue to James's moral and symbolic intention at the end of the
book is apparent in his description of Isabel's journey northward to
see Ralph Touchett, who is dying. Her love for him has led her to
make the journey; her awareness of his love for her has been reinforced
by Mme. Merle's final thrust: Ralph has endowed Isabel with her
fortune, Mme. Merle tells her. But, just as in the case of Milly Theale
and Densher, Ralph's love will be her real inheritance, not the seventy
thousand pounds. As she rides, she puts together many memories. The
past begins to compose itself into a structure: "The truth of things,
their mutual relations, their meaning, and for the most part their horror, rose before her with a kind of architectural vastness." Even this
awareness leaves her passive; she is not ready to do battle with her self.

Nothing seemed of use to her to-day. All purpose, all intention, was
suspended; all desire too save the single desire to reach her much-em-
bracing refuge. Gardencourt had been her starting-point, and to those
muffled chambers it was at least a temporary solution to return. She had
gone forth in her strength; she would come back in her weakness, and if
the place had been a rest to her before, it would be a sanctuary now.

She envied Ralph his dying, for if one were thinking of rest that was the most perfect of all. To cease utterly, to give it all up and not know anything more—the idea was as sweet as the vision of a cool bath in a marble tank, in a darkened chamber, in a hot land.

She had moments indeed in her journey from Rome which were almost as good as being dead. She sat in her corner, so motionless, so passive, simply with the sense of being carried, so detached from hope and regret, that she recalled to herself one of those Etruscan figures couched upon the receptacle of their ashes.

Isabel, with her "sense of being carried" from the scene of her encounter with herself in Rome to her "starting-point," which is now a "sanctuary," reminds us strongly of Brydon in *The Jolly Corner*. She is traversing the path between the same extremes, undergoing a kind of death as she does so. Gardencourt and its fostering love, the Palazzo Roccanera and its image of her selfishness, are in her case the extremities of the "tube or tunnel" of the Galerie d'Apollon passage. James is at pains to establish her inability, at this stage in her life, to realize fully the meaning of her movement between these extremes.

Deep in her soul—deeper than any appetite for renunciation—was the sense that life would be her business for a long time to come. And at moments there was something inspiring, almost enlivening, in the conviction. It was a proof of strength—it was a proof she should some day be happy again. It couldn't be she was to live only to suffer; she was still young, after all, and a great many things might happen to her yet. To live only to suffer—only to feel the injury of life repeated and enlarged —it seemed to her that she was too valuable, too capable for that. Then she wondered if it were vain and stupid to think so well of herself. When had it ever been a guarantee to be valuable? Wasn't all history full of the destruction of precious things? Wasn't it much more probable that if one were fine one would suffer? It involved then perhaps an admission that one had a certain grossness; but Isabel recognised, as it passed before her eyes, the quick vague shadow of a long future. She should never escape; she should last to the end. Then the middle years wrapped her about again and the grey curtain of her indifference closed her in.

Isabel's flickering perception of a "certain grossness" in her composition is not a sufficient recognition of the extremes between which mankind moves. Not until the "middle years" have ended is a full recognition of these extremes possible. The important emblematic concept of the "middle years" may be introduced by a quotation from the elder James. His theme here is the familiar one of the need to get over our selfish conviction that appearances are absolute, and may be owned or used to give us moral ascendancy over others: "Thus, reason emancipated from sense, or what is the same thing enlightened by revelation, disowns our *a priori* reasoning, and pronounces nature an altogether subjective divine work enforced in the exclusive interest of man's spiritual evolution; just as the moral control I exert over myself is a subjective work on my part enforced by my objective regard for society, or my sense of human fellowship; just as an artist's education and discipline—which often are nothing more than his physical and intellectual penury and moral compression—are a needful subjective preparation for his subsequent objective or aesthetic expansion."

The American as a Young Lady

by Christof Wegelin

Isabel's uninformed vitality is in sharp contrast with the studied formality of Osmond. Meeting him when her senses are charmed and her fancy stirred by her first experience of Italy, she is touched by "an indefinable beauty" in what seems to be his quiet devotion to private values. Her sense that he is "helpless and ineffectual" arouses in her a maternal tenderness and a desire to act with her "charged hands" as his good "providence." Very much like Ralph Touchett, when he puts money in *her* purse, she anticipates in her marriage to Osmond an "infinite vista of multiplied life"—a vista which before long she finds, however, turned into a "dark, narrow alley with a dead wall at the end." For everything in Osmond is pose; "his culture, his cleverness, his amenity"--all hide an appalling egotism. His contempt for the world turns out to be the shabbiest kind of snobbery. His deeply calculated effects, though produced by no vulgar means, have after all the vulgarest of motives. He is in sum the very antithesis of herself. Under his touch, she comes to feel, everything withers, under his look everything spoils; his very presence is a blight. Her way of looking at life, the very fact of her "having a mind of her own at all," is a personal offense to him, and he comes to hate her with the deep-seated antagonism of death for life. For, worse than a mere snob, he is the incarnate negation of the living spirit and, in his efforts to cut Isabel down to his own measure, guilty—like Hawthorne's Ethan Brand and Chillingworth—of the "unpardonable sin" of tampering with "the sanctity of the human heart." More and more, as Isabel's eyes open to all this, the sinister note increases and throws the shadow of a deep corruption over all that has seemed exquisite.

It is important to remember that Osmond is not a European but an American expatriate. James emphasizes this in a significant passage, put in the mouth of Madame Merle, his accomplice and herself one of the "wretched set." She speaks with the cold lucidity which comes

"*The American as a Young Lady.*" *From* The Image of Europe in Henry James *by Christof Wegelin (Dallas: Southern Methodist University Press, 1958), pp. 72–78. Copyright © 1958 by Southern Methodist University Press. Reprinted by permission of the publisher.*

from experience. "If we're not good Americans we're certainly poor Europeans," she tells Isabel. They have no "natural place" in Europe, no roots in the soil; at best they are collectors, devoting themselves, as Madame Merle herself does, to "some rather good old damask," or measuring their lives, as Osmond does, by the purchase of "an old silver crucifix at a bargain"—activities which are a special form of the failing peculiar to Americans in Europe, the taking of the form for the thing, illustrated already in the social snobbery of the American matrons in "Daisy Miller" or the cultural snobbery of Mrs. Church in "The Pension Beaurepas." It is also the cause of Isabel's initial failure to see the utter emptiness hidden under Osmond's superficial refinement. In Osmond it takes the form of a cultivation of tradition so perverted that he tells Isabel, if one does not have one, "one must immediately proceed to make it." And indeed she finds that he has "a very large collection" of traditions though from what source derived she cannot learn. Philip Rahv has pointed out the significance of Osmond as "a cultural type," as a portrait of the American intellectual, in whom a "residue of 'colonial' feeling" betrays itself by a tendency "to take literally" what his European counterpart is "likely to take metaphorically and imaginatively." It is all the more surprising that Rahv can speak of Osmond as "virtually a European," which indeed he is not.

For James is careful to distinguish between the American and the European antagonists of the American girl—from "Daisy Miller" to *The Golden Bowl,* where the distinction is a central part of his theme. In *The Portrait of a Lady* it is dramatized in the mutual antipathy of Osmond and Lord Warburton. Though the traditionalism of both represents a threat to the freedom of Isabel's spirit, their relations to tradition differ fundamentally. Osmond is deeply corrupt, deeply false. His traditionalism is "altogether a thing of forms, a conscious, calculated attitude," designed to cover his lack of individual substance. His seclusion on his hilltop in a villa filled with bibelots but empty of people is a symbol of his expatriation not merely from America but from all human community, from which traditions spring and which, above all, they serve. His perversion is underlined by the fact that his traditions not only take no account of such fundamental moral values as simple "decency" but actually include things so "hideously unclean" as to make Isabel feel like pushing "back her skirts." All this adds up to a sinister villainy which the picture of Lord Warburton wholly lacks. Warburton is not false simply because he is not rootless. The traditions which the other pretends to, he possesses securely, legitimately—which is the reason why Osmond desires him so immensely as a husband for his daughter. For her illegitimacy and his attempt to force her into

the marriage with the nobleman are more than a convenience of plot;
they are both symbolic of Osmond's relation to human society.

Yet, Osmond's corruption is of course not the result of his being an
American. What it illustrates is the danger which Europe exposes
Americans to. It is a danger inherent in the very process of ordering
experience significantly—the danger that the order, the form, which
results from the action of the spirit on experience, becomes frozen and
self-sufficient and finally imprisons the very spirit which gave it birth.
It is the danger typical of Europe, where the past lingers not only in
the form of ruins and associations but in the form also of institutions
which tend to perpetuate themselves even when their reason for being
if not their meaning is antiquated. Emerson's rejection of the authority of books or of the single Revelation are examples of the American
criticism of such frozen forms in the fields of philosophy and religion.
The contrast between natural and artificial aristocracy is an example
of it in the field of social and political thought which James, as we
have seen, used in some of his earliest tales and of which a trace lingers
in Isabel's relation to Lord Warburton.

Her reasons for refusing the Englishman's proposal indeed go to
the very center of James's vision of international contrast. It is not that
she objects to the "aristocratic life"; it is rather that her notions of it
differ from Warburton's. She thinks of it as "simply the union of great
knowledge with great liberty," and it is for her liberty that she fears.
Not that Warburton would imprison her as Osmond tries to do. There
is no doubt of his consideration, his kindness; there is nothing in the
least sinister about him. Yet she regards his proposal somehow as the
design of "a territorial, a political, a social magnate" to draw her into
a "system," the system of which his sisters are such charming but such
ominously pale products.

Lord Warburton's misfortune is that his eminence lies in a "collection of attributes and powers" independent of his individual character,
no matter how appealing *that* may be. In social and political terms he
is a nobleman of birth; in James's psychological terms he is the expen-
sive product of cultivation and therefore demands consideration which
Isabel does not have the patience to give. She is used to judging people
on the basis of "character and wit," on the basis of the question
whether they please "her sublime soul"—according to rules too simple
to serve as a measure of Warburton's qualifications. In a word, marriage to him fails "to support any enlightened prejudice in favour of
the free exploration of life"; there is "something stiff and stupid" in
the system which has made him—all of which is borne in upon her
with emphatic energy by a letter from Caspar Goodwood burning in
her pocket at the very time Warburton makes his plea. Goodwood,

though he too threatens her liberty, respresents a power which is in no degree a matter of his "advantages" but entirely a matter of the spirit which sits "in his clear-burning eyes like some tireless watcher at a window." And the memory of *that* power is fatal to Warburton's hopes.

The American manufacturer, engineer, mover of men, and the English Lord represent qualities which James considered more and more as typical of America and Europe. But it is important to see that they represent these qualities in a neutral equilibrium of positive and negative, that each satisfies where the other does not, that if in Warburton the man is smothered by the "system," Goodwood shows his appetites "too simply and artlessly"; that if Warburton's virtues are too much cultivated, Goodwood's are not cultivated enough. For Amercan vitality and European discipline both had alike their potentials for good and evil. Nor does James's international fiction rest, as some critics have asserted, on a distinction between moral and aesthetic values, between "cultural" inferiority but "moral" superiority in America and their opposites in Europe. In fact, wherever such explanations are attempted, the simplification leads to more or less flagrant distortions and misreadings of the moral significance of individual characters. Art and life are in James's view of things much too closely related, "the house of life and the palace of art," as he recalls in *A Small Boy and Others,* became at an early time too "mixed and interchangeable" to allow so simple an opposition between moral and aesthetic values.

How close their relation was for him a story like "The Figure in the Carpet" makes clear: "Literature was a game of skill, and skill meant courage, and courage meant honour, and honour meant passion, meant life." Even more forthright, certainly more personal, is a letter to H. G. Wells: "It is art that *makes* life," James wrote, "and I know of no substitute whatever for the force and beauty of its process." Wells answered that he could "read sense into" this statement only by assuming that James was using *art* "for every conscious human activity." "I use the word," Wells added, "for a research and attainment that is technical and special"—and nothing could have formed a clearer contrast with the intimate relation James saw between art and life, and with the organic relation of form and content which derives from it. Consciousness is, ultimately, the soul of James's art, in which "force and beauty," the moral and the aesthetic, become one. For him, "the 'moral' sense of a work of art," as he said in the preface to *The Portrait of a Lady,* depended directly on "the amount of felt life concerned in producing it." And in the preface to "The Lesson of the Master," which is perhaps his most extended single discourse on the subject, he defined the work of the artist, the "intelligent painter of life," as the midwife assistance he gives at the birth of "true meanings." Stephen Dedalus went forth to encounter "the reality of experience" and in the smithy of his soul to forge "the uncreated conscience" of his race. It is what James, too—hesitantly and without the megalomania—again and again set out to do.

His view of the process of art, moreover, was closely paralleled by his view of the process of history, both being integral to his view of life. If the virtue of art was to create "true meanings," historical experience, too, made for order, for form—for the manners, conventions, traditions governing society. These results of the continuity of European experience, of European history "as a still felt past," therefore, are in James's view by no means necessarily inimical to life. They need not smother the spirit; they may liberate it. This, in *The Portrait of a Lady,* is the meaning of the contrast between Osmond, who attempts to stifle Isabel's freedom, and Ralph Touchett, also a "Europeanized American," who provides her with freedom in order to see the promise of her spirit fulfilled. And the dual nature of convention is made explicit in the crucial chapter (XLII) in which Isabel analyzes the mistake she has made in marrying Osmond: "He had told her he loved the conventional," and it had seemed to her "a noble declaration" of his love of "harmony and order and decency and of all the stately offices of life." But with "incredulous terror," as time passes, Isabel discovers that the house of Osmond's thought is a house of darkness and suffocation to which his "beautiful mind" gives neither light nor air, a prison of the spirit or its tomb, instead of, as she thought, a noble mansion which it has built and in which it lives. For Osmond has divorced convention and tradition from life.

He and, to a minor extent, Lord Warburton, then, represent the danger inherent in the European emphasis on order. But a similar danger inheres also in the America which James contrasted with this Europe. The ultimate good in James's view of things, as we have seen, is the awareness which results from the full life, the kind of awareness which is central in the art which "*makes* life, makes interest, makes importance." And while James's images of America are rarely without the vital energy which constitutes the needed impulse for living fully, yet this energy—like the European sense of form—has potentialities for harm as well as for profit. Its promise may be broken. It, too, may turn tyrannical; it, too, may corrupt if, refusing to submit to the creative discipline of the spirit, it explodes in sheer mindless activity.

The Flaw in the Portrait

by Marion Montgomery

Professor Oscar Cargill in his re-examination of James's *Portrait of a Lady* (*Modern Fiction Studies,* Spring 1957) concludes: "There is not an accidental relationship or a badly proportioned one in *The Portrait of a Lady.* Judged on purely aesthetic grounds, the book is possibly matchless." James himself thought well of the book's form. It has, he says in his Preface, "a structure reared with an 'architectural' competence, as Turgenieff would have said, that makes it, to the author's own sense, the most proportioned of his productions after *The Ambassadors.*" And, as Professor Cargill points out, Professor Millet has abstracted the structure as a dramatic form consisting of three acts and an epilogue.

When one looks at the blueprint of the novel with James and Millet and Cargill, the novel is impressive, but then so is the structural blueprint of a sonnet. However, the blueprint, beautiful in itself, is not the novel and is not sufficient to justify a claim to aesthetic perfection. And the novel is not a blueprint; it is not even the complete building: it is the complete building with people living in it. It seems evident that James, after he got into the writing of *The Portrait,* forgot that the novelist, unlike the architect, does not necessarily build his novel according to his preconceived blueprint: he consults the inhabitants of the novel he is building and he modifies the structure as he builds, particularly when he is dealing with an Isabel Archer.

I say forgot, for James does not start immediately with the structure he finally imposes, a structure that is in the end disproportionate. His starting point was, he says, "the character and aspect of a particular engaging young woman, to which all the elements of a 'subject,' certainly of a setting, were to need to be superadded." The subject is not, however, "superadded." It is inherent in that aspect of the young woman, Isabel Archer, which makes her engaging to James. It is Isabel's concern for freedom as she is gradually, tragically, confronted

---

"The Flaw in the Portrait" by Marion Montgomery. From The University of Kansas City Review, *XXVI (March, 1960), 215–20. Copyright © 1960 by the University of Kansas City Press. Reprinted by permission of the editor.*

by freedom's restrictions which is the novel's subject and which calls characters and the inevitable setting into being from the storehouse of James's mind. The point is that these elements are not "super-added," but, happily, evolved. A brief survey of Isabel's character will, perhaps, help demonstrate a serious aesthetic flaw which results from James's ultimate failure to let structure as well as subject, characters, and setting evolve.

The male characters of *The Portrait* are, with the exception of Osmond and Caspar Goodwood, particularly vulnerable to the charm with which Isabel wears her freedom. Her innocent independence attracts the old, infirm Mr. Touchett. It is an independence which can assert itself equally to his unsympathetic wife and to him without estranging either, and so he is enthralled. It is her free and independent spirit which also attracts Ralph Touchett, an equally free-spirited young person, though one more wisely sober than Isabel since his freedom is ironically shadowed by a frail body. Isabel is not one whose individuality is to be overcome by sympathy for a sensitive and sickly young man. Nor is it overcome by the glamor of a Lord Warburton. Consequently both Ralph and Lord Warburton are fascinated; both fall in love with her. So strong and innocent is this desire for freedom in Isabel that Lord Warburton almost immediately proposes marriage, and Ralph persuades Mr. Touchett to will Isabel sufficient funds to exercise her grand conception of freedom so that she may fly above the world of necessity which infringes upon freedom.

But if Lord Warburton, Ralph, Mr. Touchett, and even Isabel herself do not detect in Isabel's love of independence the seed of her destruction, the women in the novel do. Mrs. Touchett perceives in Isabel quite early an inclination which Isabel confuses with social and spiritual freedom. Mrs. Touchett calls it wilfulness, and she sees it reflected in Isabel's refusal to be restricted by the social mores to which Mrs. Touchett wishes to expose her. Nevertheless, she is sufficiently impressed with Isabel to respect her wilfulness and to take her abroad to give her native independence a grander stage on which to learn control of itself. Likewise the indomitable Henrietta Stackpole sees in Isabel's independence a threat to happiness. And it is finally Madame Merle who sees in Isabel's conception of freedom a naiveté which may be used against her.

As we first see Isabel, then, her independence is a natural disposition which even the sophisticated Mrs. Touchett appreciates. But under the pressure of others' appreciation and manipulation of it—Ralph's, Mr. Touchett's, Warburton's, Madame Merle's—Isabel becomes aware of independence as a virtue and begins to cast a romantic light around it. "If there's a thing in the world I'm fond of . . . it's my personal independence," she tells Caspar Goodwood, who is skeptical of her attitude. "A swift carriage, a dark night, rattling with four horses over roads that one can't see—that's my idea of happiness," she later argues to the pragmatic Henrietta, who is likewise skeptical of Isabel's conception of the ends of freedom. It is but a short step from consciousness of freedom as a virtue to the romantic expansion of freedom into a vice, a step which prepares Isabel's downfall.

Isabel has not, in fact, realized the implications of freedom. She is suddenly confronted with a fortune left her by Mr. Touchett. "A large fortune means freedom," she says, "and I am afraid of that." She is afraid because in her first innocent championing of freedom she has never had to ask herself what freedom is. Now she does not really wish to know. We are told that her ideal, like that of Emma Bovary, is "a thing to believe in, not to see—a matter of faith, not of experience." In short, Isabel is happy so long as she appears capable of flight, so long as she hasn't wings which force her into flight. So that having gained financial freedom, she turns to another and remoter freedom. Her first touchstones (perhaps the family name is supposed to suggest this role) are the Touchetts, who appear too restrictive to freedom now. She has been sheltered and nurtured by the intellectual freedom of Ralph and the social freedom of Mr. Touchett. She is suddenly released from their shadows by the gift of financial freedom from Mr. Touchett.

And now Isabel rejects the freedom she has enjoyed under the protection of the Touchetts for a vague romantic impulse. Her new ideal she finds personified in Osmond, of whom Ralph and Mrs. Touchett disapprove. Their disapproval seems to her a threat to freedom, so that she flees more swiftly to Osmond. After Isabel's and Ralph's argument over Osmond, Isabel says, "I've only one ambition—to be free to follow out a good feeling. I had others once, but they've passed away." And so intent is she on this dream that she can not see Osmond as Ralph correctly sees him: "Under the guise of caring only for intrinsic values Osmond lived exclusively for the world. . . . Everything he did was *pose—pose* so subtly considered that if one were not on the lookout one mistook it for impulse."

Isabel does not even see the obvious warning in the person of Pansy, whose freedom has been completely destroyed. Pansy is the perfect image of Osmond's desire, paraded by him before the unperceptive Isabel. Isabel, angered by the Touchetts' interference and misled by her pride, destroys social, intellectual, financial liberties by marrying Osmond. It is with an extremely unsettling shock that she comes to realize that Osmond is intent upon control of her fortune and her mind. She has been of a free and open nature and therefore has been an easy mark for the Iago-like Osmond.

At this point in her career there seems to be some confusion in

James's conception of Isabel. He repeatedly tells us that she is not ready to assume responsibility for her error of judgment. "I have mentioned how passionately she needed to feel that her unhappiness should not have come to her through her own fault." But her words and actions show her determined to blame herself. She does tell Henrietta that she is not willing to publish her mistake, but more importantly she says, "One must accept one's deeds. I married him before the world; I was perfectly free; it was impossible to do anything more deliberate." Consequently she turns to self-torture in penance.

Isabel's mistake has been a superficial judgment of Osmond in the light of her new freedom, a freedom which had seen the true aristocratic life as transcending the social and financial relationships so sanely dear to Mrs. Touchett. The true aristocratic life is "simply the union of great knowledge with great liberty; the knowledge would give one a sense of duty and the liberty a sense of enjoyment." Repeating Ralph's mistake in judgment, Isabel has thought that by bringing her money to Osmond, whom she thinks a man of great knowledge, she will have conferred upon him the great liberty she thinks she possesses.

When Isabel's marriage is a total failure, when she has lost her liberty, an important turning point in her history is reached. She turns desperately to duty, which has only fleetingly concerned her before. She romantically exaggerates duty so that it means doing Osmond's wishes whether right or wrong. She furthers Warburton's suit to Pansy against all her better feelings. "Suffering, with Isabel, was an active condition," we are told. It is this morbid sense of duty which prevents her breaking free of Osmond at the insistence of Henrietta, Ralph, and Caspar, three people who understand duty and freedom far better than she does. It is the same morbid sense of duty which makes her feel compassion for Madame Merle, who deceives her, since in deceiving Isabel and ruining her life, Madame Merle is but practicing maternal duty to Pansy. It is likewise this morbid sense of duty which makes her encourage Pansy to stay in the convent, marry whomever her father chooses, in short, to give up all her freedom.

Isabel puts an emphasis upon the marriage vows far heavier than her piety or conscience will explain. "Marriage meant that in such a case as this, when one had to choose, one chose as a matter of course for one's husband." So that in going from one romantic extreme to the other, from vague freedom to blind duty, Isabel sets the stage for one final, inevitable difficulty. She receives word that Ralph is dying. Her duty to Ralph and her duty to her enslaving husband are hard to reconcile. Ralph, in sending for her, has tried a final time to show her that freedom and duty are compatible, to teach her a way to freedom through compassionate duty. But still she hesitates. It is only when she learns of Osmond's affair with Madame Merle—when she realizes that Osmond has not been a dutiful husband—that she feels justified in going to Ralph.

And when she arrives at Ralph's bedside, he realizes that she will not gain her freedom in the end. "I should like to stay—as long as seems right," she says. Ralph replies, "As seems right—? . . . Yes, you think a great deal about that." Yet Isabel knows no more what makes duty right than she knows what constitutes freedom. After Ralph's death Caspar Goodwood tries a final time to induce her to stay with him. "It would be an insult to you to assume that you care for the look of the thing, for what people will say, for the bottomless idiocy of the world." Caspar is right; she is not concerned for the look of things. But though she is drawn to Caspar, she flees freedom, going back to Italy and Osmond and the self-inflicted punishment she insists upon for her failure to understand and use the freedom given by the Touchetts. Isabel commits a spiritual suicide as Emma Bovary commits physical suicide. And the ending, over which so much controversy rages, would carry the sense of inevitable reality were it not for the flaw. As the novel stands, the conclusion seems a romantically conceived unhappy ending, an almost heroic renunciation, but a renunciation that appears unjustified.

We have been concerned with the conflict between freedom and duty in the character of Isabel Archer. Let us turn finally to consider the conflict of James's artistic freedom of character and what he considered his artistic duty to form. Having conceived such a character as Isabel Archer, James set her going to see what actions she would attract to her by virtue of her character, the consequence of which act we have just concerned ourselves with. But though he sets Isabel going, giving her the freedom to develop, he is extremely anxious lest his material escape his control. He wishes to reveal his Isabel gradually through form and style. His task is complicated by the fact that his central character is not constant, that she is capable of change, of actions which the author cannot positively foresee at the outset. In other words, when James sets Isabel Archer loose to collect the world of a novel around her, he is certain only that she is a person concerned with freedom, that her understanding of freedom is a superficial one, and that through this defect she will lose her freedom.

On the basis of this knowledge he decides that the climax will naturally occur at the point where Isabel loses her freedom, that is, when she marries Osmond. And so James determines the general organization and proportions of the novel according to this conception of the novel's action. His concern for structure, his desire to foreshorten climax so that rising action equals falling action, tempts him to hold a thumb on Isabel, to make her wait till her house is almost built before he lets her in to furnish it.

But such a character as Isabel Archer approached as James wishes her to be approached is going to have something to say about the floor plan itself. However much James may have felt the climax of the novel to be Isabel's marriage, it is not so. The marriage is no more the climax than the murder of Duncan is the climax of *Macbeth*. Such an assignment of the climax is contrary to the point of view which James follows. For we are to witness the effects of events upon Isabel, as James says, and these effects are to lend significance to the actions—not the actions to the effects. Isabel's marriage is perhaps a climax to the other characters in the book—particularly to such persons as Ralph and Caspar. However, we are not supposed to be primarily interested by their reactions but by Isabel's.

When the story resumes after the marriage, and after a lapse of three years, we are shown an Isabel Archer drastically changed. We have, in fact, a second portrait unveiled; but we have not seen it painted as we did the first. There is a great effort to account for the change through long expository paragraphs and through equally long reflections of some of the characters. But the most dramatic part of Isabel's history and the most crucial period of her life so far as justification of her ultimate decision to return to Osmond is concerned is presented in an incomplete and undramatic fashion. Furthermore, the climax of the book, intrinsic in Isabel's nature and in the author's point of view, comes when she is completely disillusioned upon discovering that Madame Merle is Pansy's mother. For at this point freedom and duty are both turned to dust for Isabel, the character whose fortunes we are asked to follow to catastrophe.

Rather oddly James writes in his notebook just before composing the sections following Isabel's marriage, "If the last five parts of the story appear crowded this will be rather a good defect in consideration of the perhaps too great diffuseness of the earlier portions." He is trapped by the general form imposed upon the material too early in the writing, by the fact that he has already published those first sections in serial form, and, primarily, because he does not wish to give up the artificial scheme of making rising action equal falling action. Consequently the most powerful part of the book does not achieve its potential because of its compression and because the natural climax is not made the most of. As the notebook quotation shows, James is defending the flaw even before the flaw is finally committed, and his defense is based on the novel's abstracted structure, upon the beauty of the blueprint.

In the same notebook passage quoted above, there appears a statement which indicates that James was not fully aware of the great possibilities of his character. "The weakness of the whole story is that it is too exclusively psychological—that it depends too little on incident." On the contrary, James's material seems as dramatically potent as that which Shakespeare uses in *Othello,* particularly when one considers that it is to be given treatment in a novel. The same notebook passage shows James still speculating about Isabel's future actions at this midpoint in the composition. In itself this uncertainty would constitute no insurmountable obstacle to the satisfactory completion of the book. But James attempts, like Balzac, to give his character the freedom to find her own way while at the same time he is insisting, as Flaubert would do, on forcing her to act within a predetermined framework. The general structure, "superadded," is not congenial to the character nor to the actions she attracts. James's instinctive artistry, which demands sufficient freedom of form, is at odds with his dogmatic principles which demand strict form. He does not allow himself a freedom of execution worthy of his conception. The result is that he gives two portraits of Isabel Archer rather than one, the first being considerably out of proportion to the second.

The Fearful Self

by Tony Tanner

I

The feeling which Isabel Archer most consistently experiences is fear. She is frightened by Warburton's offer, of Caspar Goodwood's persistence, and Gilbert Osmond's anger; she is frightened of sexual passion, of her unexpected wealth, of her 'freedom'; but beneath all these specific apprehensions there is, she admits, a deeper, radical fear —fear of herself. Seeing that it is a self which can misread Osmond so disastrously and make such a profoundly mistaken choice then, we may say, she has good grounds for her fear. But her fear, her error, and her final resolution are, it seems to me, crucial stages on a psychic journey which forms the very heart of the novel. This journey is the journey of an uncommitted, undefined self which sets out to find the right house to live in and the right partner to live with. A house— because the undefined self needs a defining shape: a partner—because the self can only realize what it is, by seeing itself reflected in the chosen and respected eyes of another; in selecting a partner it is selecting the gaze and regard which will assure it of its own reality and value. Putting it very crudely, Isabel Archer chooses the wrong house and the wrong partner. It is the full nature of this error—and her subsequent actions—that I wish to explore. But first I should like to make it clear that if I tend to treat characters, events, and buildings as being 'emblematic' (Quentin Anderson's word), this does not mean that I am insensitive to the more realistic qualities of the novel which are praised, for example, by F. R. Leavis in *The Great Tradition*. I certainly do not wish to suggest that the book is something aridly schematized and drained of the opaque complexity of life in the interests of abstract meanings. The life is there: Isabel remains a hauntingly authentic and elusive character moving through vivid and tangible territories. But James has so selected and arranged his realistic data, and has so saturated it with deeper implications, that Isabel's

"*The Fearful Self*" by Tony Tanner. *From* The Critical Quarterly, *VII* (*Autumn, 1965*), *205–219. Copyright* © *1965 by Tony Tanner. Reprinted by permission of the author and publisher.*

journey is also an analogue of the journey of the inquiring self seeking realization and identity. Everyone she meets, every house she enters, all are detailed, plausible, recognizably of the world. But they are also significant steps of an inward quest which far transcends the social realism of a young American girl living in late nineteenth century Europe. In this essay I shall be stressing the inner quest more than the outer realism—but of course, either without the other would be an immeasurably poorer thing. To suggest the full significance of Isabel's error I shall be considering some of the characters and then some of the architecture. But first I want to make a general point about the Jamesian world which I can best clarify by introducing a quotation from Kant (not, indeed, suggesting any direct influence, even though Henry James Senior studied Kant fairly thoroughly). Kant asserts that 'in the realm of ends everything has either a value or a worth. What has a value has a substitute which can replace it as its equivalent; but whatever is, on the other hand, exalted above all values, and thus lacks an equivalent . . . has no merely relative value, that is, a price, but rather an inner worth, that is, dignity. Now morality is the condition in accordance with which alone a reasonable being can be an end in himself, because only through morality is it possible to be an autonomous member of the realm of ends. Hence morality, and humanity, in so far as it is capable of morality, can alone possess dignity.' This idea is compactly summarized in his second categorical imperative. 'So act as to treat humanity, whether in thine own person or in that of any other, in every case as an end withal, never as a means whereby.' And this key statement was probably influenced, as Ernst Cassirer has suggested, by Rousseau's maxim: "Man is too noble a being to serve simply as the instrument for others, and he must not be used for what suits them without consulting also what suits himself. . . . It is never right to harm a human soul for the Advantage of others."

I have introduced these quotations because I think they offer useful terms with which to outline James's moral universe. Imagine two worlds. One is the world of ends in which everything and everyone has an intrinsic worth and they are all respected for what they are. That is, literally, they are regarded as ends in themselves. This is the moral world. In the other world, everything and everyone is regarded as a means, nothing is considered as having a fixed inherent worth but only what Kant calls a 'value.' This is misleading since we tend to use 'value' to imply 'worth,' so let us say 'price,' i.e., a market value which may change as appetites change, as opposed to an inner spiritual value, a permanent immutable worth. In this lower world of means, people only look at each other in the light of how they can use people, manipulate them, exploit or coerce them in the interests of some personal desire or appetite, or indeed mutilate and shape them to fit the dictates of a theory or a whim. In this world people see other people only as things or instruments, and they work to appropriate them as suits their own ambition. The world of means is a world of rampant egoism, while the world of ends is the realm of true morality and love. These two worlds are effectively the upper and lower parts of James's moral world. And what happens to Isabel Archer is that while she thinks she is ascending towards the world of ends, she is in fact getting more deeply involved in the world of means. The shocking knowledge she has to confront after her marriage is that she is "a woman who has been made use of" as the Countess Gemini puts it. She who thought herself so free, so independent, a pure disciple of the beautiful, now has to face up to the 'dry staring fact that she had been an applied hung-up tool, as senseless and convenient as mere shaped wood and iron.' She, of all people, finds herself trapped in the world of instruments and things. Seeking a world of disinterested appreciation, she falls into a world of calculating appropriation. How does an error of such magnitude come about?

II

Isabel Archer's character has been amply analyzed by many other critics so all I want to do is stress that from the outset her approach to life is very romantic, idealistic, and theoretic. 'Isabel Archer was a young person of many theories; her imagination was remarkably active' as James tells us clearly enough. And Henrietta Stackpole is certainly correct when she says to Isabel: "The peril for you is that you live too much in the world of your own dreams." What these dreams consist of we know right from the start: 'she spent half her time in thinking of beauty and bravery and magnanimity; she had a fixed determination to regard the world as a place of brightness, of free expansion, of irresistible action . . . she was always planning out her development, desiring her perfection, observing her progress.' Thus, she views the world as a benevolent sphere which will be plastic to her theories of 'free expansion' and 'irresistible action.' She seems unprepared for any harsh encounter with all that indifferent otherness which is not the self, which is not amenable to the self, and which may well prove cruel and hostile to the self. More dangerously, it is hard to see how she intends to put her theories of self-development into practice. What will that expansion and action consist of? As we soon realize, her most characteristic response in the real world is one of refusal and rejection. Like many another character in American fiction much of her energy goes into avoiding any commitment which might serve to define and arrest her. She is generally in favor of 'the free ex-

ploration of life' and yet she shrinks from any of the solid offers that
life holds forth. Caspar Goodwood suggests oppression, coercion, and
constraint on the plain physical level. Lord Warburton with his complex social relations and obligations suggests immobilization on the
social level. If she rejects the first out of a distinct disinclination to
enter a firm physical embrace, she rejects the second on 'theoretic'
grounds because what he offers does not tally with her vague notions
of indefinite expansion. So we may say, summing up, that she rejects
the physical and the social in her theoretic pursuit of freedom, knowledge, and self-realization. Why, then, does she go on to accept Osmond? As she realizes, 'The world lay before her—she could do whatever she chose'—the Miltonic echo is deliberate, it recurs again. And
out of the whole world to choose Osmond! Notice that she is the only
character in the book who is remotely taken in by this 'sterile dilettante' as Ralph so cogently calls him. Why? When we first see her she
is reading a history of German thought; that is to say, drinking from
the very source of American transcendentalism. And when, later, she
imagines her future married life with Osmond, she feels assured of
'a future at a high level of consciousness of the beautiful.' This implies
a sort of romantic Platonism which she might well have found in her
youthful reading. She wants to exist at the heights of sheer communion
with ideal beauty. As opposed, we may say, to involving herself with
the lower levels of un-ideal actuality. From the start she tests things
and people by whether they please her 'sublime soul'; and when she
receives her fortune, the vast amount of money gives her 'to her imagination, a certain ideal beauty.' Isabel's instinct for the actual is as cur-
tailed as her longing for the ideal is exaggerated. She rejects the
sexual and social life. In marrying Osmond she thinks she is embracing the ideal. She idealizes herself, her motives for marrying, her ambitions, and Osmond himself. It is all pathetically wrong. But as Mrs.
Touchett shrewdly says: "there's nothing in life to prevent her marrying Mr. Osmond if only she looks at him in a certain way." Looking
at him in her own way—romantically, theoretically (she 'invented a
fine theory about Gilbert Osmond'), consulting her yearning for a life
lived on the ideal level—Osmond seems perfectly suited to Isabel's
needs.

Among other things, then, her mistake is the result of a radical failure of vision: idealizing too much, she has perceived all too little. But
more than that, Osmond is exactly what a large part of Isabel wants.
He seems to offer release from the troubling life of turbulent passions;
he seems to offer a life dedicated to the appreciation of ideal beauty.
As we well know, Osmond merely regards Isabel as worthy 'to figure
in his collection of choice objects'; but consider how Isabel feels about
herself just before her marriage and at the height of her confidence in

herself: 'she walked in no small shimmering splendour. She only felt older—ever so much, and as if she were "worth more" for it, like some curious piece in an antiquary's collection.' And she enjoys this feeling. It is hard to resist the conclusion that a part of her—the theorizing, idealizing part—is quite prepared to be placed in Osmond's collection. The lady is half willing to be turned into a portrait. And, given her temperament, there is much to be said for becoming a work of art. It offers a reprieve from the disturbing ordeals awaiting the self in the mire of the actual. Osmond is a student of the 'exquisite' and we discover how cruel and sterile that can be. But in her own way so is Isabel. She speaks honest words about their marriage: 'They had attempted only one thing, but that one thing was to have been exquisite.' In some ways Osmond is as much a collaborator as a deceiver.

Although there are hints of the proper villain about Osmond (James perhaps goes a little too far by revealing that Osmond's favorite author is Machiavelli), he is in fact a curiously hollow, insubstantial man: "no career, no name, no position, no fortune, no past, no future, no anything" as Madame Merle says. Perhaps this apparent lightness, this seemingly empty detachment from the world is more attractive to Isabel than the solid identity, the heavy actuality of Goodwood and Warburton. Certainly his claim that he has renounced passional life and ordinary human attachments to pursue his high-minded study, his 'taste,' echoes something in Isabel. The paradox, of course, as Ralph sees, is 'that under the guise of caring only for intrinsic values Osmond lived exclusively for the world. Far from being its master as he pretended to be, he was its very humble servant, and the degree of its attention was his only measure of success.' He pretends to be a devotee of the ideal, to have renounced the base world. This is what draws Isabel. But to care so totally and uncritically for forms, taste, convention ("I'm convention itself" he revealingly admits) is to be absolutely enslaved to mere appearances, never questioning essences or the intrinsic worth of things. This, precisely, makes him a dedicated inhabitant of the world of means. He has renounced the lived life of instinct and action not, like Ralph, the better to appreciate its intrinsic values, but in order to give himself over entirely to calculated surface effects. How far he will take this is of course revealed by what he does to his daughter Pansy. It is the same thing as what he wants to do to Isabel—to turn her into a reflector of himself, utterly devoid of any spontaneous life of her own. Isabel of course, having stronger and richer stuff in her, can resist. But Pansy shows the process all but complete. All her natural vitality and spontaneity have been quietly suffocated to be replaced by a perfected puppet-like behavior which does not *express* Pansy's own inner life, but simply *reflects* Osmond's taste. Such a total appropriation of another person's life for egotistical

ends is of course the cardinal Jamesian sin. But there is something in
Isabel herself which is not so remote from Osmond's disposition. At
one point we read that she was 'interested' (a neutral word) to watch
Osmond 'playing theoretic tricks on the delicate organism of his daughter.' She should be interested, for she has spent her whole life playing
theoretic tricks on her own organism. Osmond is an egotist, but so, we
are told, is Isabel: he is cold and dry, but so is she: he pays excessive
attention to appearances rather than realities, and up to a point so
does she (I will return to this): he prefers art to life, and so does
she: he has more theories than feelings, more ideals than instincts,
and so does she. He is a collector of things, and she offers herself up to
him as a fine finished object. Isabel accepting Osmond's proposal of
marriage is the uncertain self thinking it is embracing the very image
of what it *seeks* to become. Her later shock and revulsion is the self
discovering the true worthlessness of what it *might* have become. Osmond is Isabel's anti-self. This is why, I think, James made Osmond
American when he might well have made him a cynical European en-
snaring American gullibility. He is American because Isabel is American. She of course has qualities which differentiate her sharply from
Osmond. But she also has tendencies which draw her straight to him.
He is an actualization, a projection, of some of the mixed potentialities
and aspirations of her questing, uncommitted self. He is part of her
self writ large, and when she learns to read that writing properly (she
actually refers to not having 'read him right'), she is not unnaturally
appalled.

I must here say a little about the other American 'parasite' and plot-
ter, Madame Merle. As Osmond is 'convention itself' so she is 'the great
round world itself.' She is totally devoted to the world of things—she
thinks of it in terms of 'spoils'—and she has subjected the unruliness of
authentic nature to the surface perfection of contrived manner. Isabel
is not so blind as not to be able to detect her occasional cruelty, her
subtle dishonesty, the sense she gives of 'values gone wrong.' But unlike Osmond, there is something pathetic about her, and something
which also offers a warning to Isabel. For clearly Madame Merle was,
like Isabel, first used and then abused by Osmond, and she has not
gained anything from the world even though she has devoted herself to
it. She keeps herself going by 'will,' forcing, always, the right mask for
the right occasion. But she ends up utterly dried up, unable to cry:
"you've dried up my soul" she says to Osmond (it is worth recalling
here that no less a writer than Shakespeare habitually depicted evil as
a state of desiccation, a complete lack of the very sap and tears of life).
Perhaps the saddest cry in the whole novel is Madame Merle's lament:
"Have I been so vile for nothing?" It at least attests to a vestigial
moral sense which she has deliberately subverted for the world's ends,

only to see no gains. She has been a disciple of appearances and indeed has mastered the art, but she is rewarded by being banished to America (apparently the worst fate James could conceive of for an erring character). She is a sadder case than Osmond because she knows that she is doing bad things to Isabel. Her effects are as calculated as Osmond's but at least she winces at perpetrating them. She is an almost tragic example of the scant rewards and plentiful shames awaiting those who live only for 'the world.' And it is Madame Merle who gives perhaps the most succinct expression of living in the world of means to be found in the whole book. "I don't pretend to know what people are for" she says, "I only know what I can do with them." She exactly fits Kant's (and Rousseau's) definition of the immoral world. She sees people as instruments but has no sense of their intrinsic worth: means to her hand, not ends in themselves.

In the world of Osmond and Madame Merle, self-seeking and simulation go together. They have to calculate effects: what *is,* is neglected; what *seems* is paramount. Now Isabel herself is a partial devotee of appearances. I will quote a few references to this. She has 'an unquenchable desire to please' and 'an unquenchable desire to think well of herself': thus she is 'very liable to the sin of self-esteem.' More subtly, we read of 'her desire to *look* very well and to *be* if possible even better.' A similar crucial distinction is made later: Isabel's chief dread 'was that she should *appear* narrow-minded; what she feared next afterwards was that she should really *be* so.' (My italics in both cases.) These fine hints reveal a problem of great importance for the novitiate self: which will receive more attention—appearance, or essence? For much of the early part of her travels Isabel falls into the subtle and understandable error of devoting herself to appearances. She wishes to emulate Madame Merle. She contrives to appear to Osmond as she thinks he wants her to appear; like a fine finished work of art which re-echoes and reflects his ideas and taste. In this sense Osmond *is* a man deceived, and Isabel is right to realize that she did mislead him by appearing to be what in fact she was not. That is why Isabel has a true instinct when she says she is afraid of her self. Realizing the depths of her error with regard to Osmond is also to realize that she does not know what her self is, nor what it may do. (After all there is Madame Merle, a terrible example of how the self may mutilate the self from a sense of misplaced devotion and ambition.) And indeed this is the crucial difficulty for the self. Only by engaging itself in a situation, projecting itself into the world of things and appearances, can the self realize the self (i.e., transform latent potentialities into visible realities). But once in that situation, it may find that it has chosen a position, a role, which falsifies the self. We don't know what is in us until we commit ourselves in a certain direction: then we may find that

the commitment is utterly wrong. Thus all choice may turn out to
be error and in this way the self may ruin the self. Certainly Isabel
exacerbates her chances of choosing wrong by coldly consulting her
theories, her imaginative ideals, her book-fed romanticisms; and that
wrong choice does seem to threaten years to come of waste and disap-
pointment. Seen thus, Isabel's difficulty, her error, her fate, form a
journey on which we must all, in our different ways, go. For it is only
through choice and commitment that we can find out what we are. In
this sense error is also discovery. Isabel has to close with Osmond in
order to arrive at a deeper knowledge of her self, of her distorted values, of her egotism, and of the real pain and cruelty of life. By marrying Osmond she suffers in good earnest, but she thus earns the right to
see the ghost of Gardencourt. Her consolation—and it is the supreme
one in James—is truer vision.

III

   To bring out more clearly Isabel's journey as the journey of the
developing but all-too-often erring self, I now want to move from the
characters she meets to the buildings and settings she moves through.
And first I must quote from a crucial exchange between Isabel and
Madame Merle: it comes near the end of chapter nineteen and is really
central to the whole book. Talking of an earlier suitor Isabel says: "I
don't care anything about his house" and Madame Merle replies:
"That's very crude of you. When you've lived as long as I you'll see
that every human being has his shell and that you must take the shell
into account. By the shell I mean the whole envelope of circumstances.
There's no such thing as an isolated man or woman; we're each of us
made up of some cluster of appurtenances. What shall we call our
'self'? Where does it begin? where does it end? It overflows into everything that belongs to us—and then it flows back again. I know a large
part of myself is in the clothes I choose to wear. I've a great respect for
things. One's self—for other people—is one's expression of one's self;
and one's house, one's furniture, one's garments, the books one reads,
the company one keeps—these things are all expressive."
   Now this idea that the self is only the self that we consciously create
and play at being, the self that we visibly express and project, is still
being explored by existential psychologists like Sartre (for instance in
Being and Nothingness where he discusses the waiter 'playing at being
a waiter . . . the waiter in the cafe plays with his condition in order
to *realize* it'), and by such imaginative sociologists as Erving Goffman
(his brilliant book *The Presentation of Self in Everyday Life* is very
relevant here). So Madame Merle's attitude expresses a deep truth
about our society. She has gone the whole way. She is concerned only

with the agents of expression—things, clothes, appearances, appurtenances. She reconstructs a false self to show the world. She is what she dresses to be. This is extreme: it entails the death of the soul and the ultimate disappearance of the individual inner self. As Isabel says to herself, it is difficult to imagine Madame Merle 'in any detachment or privacy, she existed only in relations . . . one might wonder what commerce she could possibly hold with her own spirit.' She is rather like Lord Mellifont in "The Private Life" who disappears when he is on his own. If you care only for appearances, you exist only when there are people to look at you.

However, in this key conversation, Isabel's answer to Madame Merle is also extreme. She says: "I know that nothing else expresses me. Nothing that belongs to me is any measure of me; everything's on the contrary a limit, a barrier, and a perfectly arbitrary one. . . . My clothes may express the dressmaker, but they don't express me. To begin with it's not my own choice that I wear them; they're imposed upon me by society." To which Madame Merle wryly answers: "Should you prefer to go without them?"

This is a classic formulation of a basic American attitude. Lionel Trilling once noted that there is something in the American temperament which wishes to resist all conditioning, all actual society, and aspires to a life which will permit the spirit to make its own terms. 'Somewhere in our mental constitution is the demand for life as pure spirit.' (See his essay "William Dean Howells" in *The Opposing Self*.) Emerson's 'Self-Reliance,' Thoreau by Walden Pond, Whitman celebrating the self—these, of course, are the classic types for the American imagination. They certainly did believe there was such a thing as the 'isolated' self, and welcomed the fact. And characters like Bartleby and Huck Finn and Augie March reveal the ineradicable suspicion of all conditioning forces, all actual fixed social situations. They refuse, opt out, move on. Like Isabel they see barriers and limits everywhere, and much of their energy goes into avoiding the shaping pressures (and appurtenances) of society. Isabel's retort is, thus, in a great American tradition. And up to a point she is right. Things and appurtenances are not identical with the self, as Osmond and Madame Merle make them. We are not what we wear. But to see everything in the actual world as sheer barrier, hindrance, and limit is also dangerous. For without any limits the self can never take on any contours, cannot become something real. The pure spirit of the self has to involve itself with the material world of things and society in order to work out an identity for itself, indeed in order to realize itself. To that extent the self must dress itself and must choose its clothes. In laying the responsibility for her clothes (i.e. her appearance, her situation etc.) on society and calling it an arbitrary imposition, Isabel is being dangerously irresponsible. For it is her error in thinking that life can be lived as pure spirit in contempt of things that leads her to mistake Osmond's attitude. The ironic result is that she puts herself in the power of a man who wants to treat *her* as a thing. James's insight here is profound. For there is indeed a dangerously close connection between an idealistic *rejection* of 'things' and an idealizing *of* 'things.' This is why Osmond is such a telling figure. In the appearance of living for the spirit in disregard of the material, he has in fact simply spiritualized the material. And James must surely have been one of the first to see into this particularly modern malaise which other American critics have mentioned in discussing modern society; namely, the confusion of the spiritual and material realms, the spiritualizing of things. James knew that things and surroundings (the shell) *were* important: there was a way of being among things which manifested the quality of the self, which enabled it to realize itself. But of course there was also a way of being among things which menaced and could destroy the self. Isabel Archer's journey is hazardous but representative: and her error no less than human.

We first see Isabel—as we last see her—in a garden. This is always an important setting in James (usually indicating a place of meditation and appreciation). Gardens are certainly important in this book. At the start of her European journey Isabel regards her inner world as a garden and indeed many of her happiest moments are spent in them. She is happiest, in particular, at Gardencourt, and the very name points to the fact that this is the locale in the book which most exudes a mood of mellow reciprocity between the civilized and the natural. But Isabel is far from appreciating it at the start of her adventures. She sees it only as romantic and picturesque. It is only much later that she appreciates that it is something more real and indeed more sacred than that. After this opening glimpse James takes us back to the house in Albany, New England, where Isabel started on her travels. The most important of many suggestive details about this house is the 'condemned door,' the entrance which 'was secured by bolts which a particularly slender little girl found it impossible to slide.' It is to be Isabel's later fate again to be locked in. Also, the windows are covered, but 'she had no wish to look out, for this would have interfered with her theory that there was a strange, unseen place on the other side—a place which became to the child's imagination, according to different moods, a region of delight or terror.' This of course expresses Isabel's whole attitude to life: her theories and imagined versions of reality are generated behind closed doors and covered windows. Instead of venturing forth she sits poring over books. One more detail is particularly prophetic: she 'had the whole house to choose from, and the room she had selected was the most depressed of its scenes.' James often used the metaphor 'the house of life' and indeed, of its many rooms, Isabel is yet to choose the darkest and most imprisoning.

If you see Isabel's quest as being at least in part a search for the right house then her reactions to Warburton and Osmond become even more revealing. When she rejects Warburton after visiting his house, Lockleigh, she puts her rejection in this way: she says she is unable "to think of your home . . . as the settled seat of my existence." As though the main thing about him was the fact that he doesn't have what she regards as the right house. Osmond's house is brilliantly described. First of all, it is on a hill-top, the best place for a person who wants to put the claims of the base world behind and live a life of ideal appreciation and detached observation. Clearly Isabel is attracted to this degree of rarefied removal. But we note that in the first, perfectly plausible, topographical description, the front of the house is deceptive. 'It was the mask, not the face of the house. It had heavy lids, but no eyes; the house in reality looked another way. . . .' This, I need hardly point out, is entirely true of its owner. Even the windows bespeak Osmond: 'their function seemed less to offer communication with the world than to defy the world to look in.' Isabel's approach to this key dwelling is laced with subtle portent, and I must quote at some length here. 'The companions drove out of the Roman Gate . . . and wound between high-walled lanes into which the wealth of blossoming orchards overdrooped and flung a fragrance, until they reached the small suburban piazza, of crooked shape, where the long brown wall of the villa occupied by Mr. Osmond formed a principal, or at least very imposing, object.' They drive into the courtyard. 'There was something grave and strong in the place; it looked somehow as if, once you were in, you would need an act of energy to get out. For Isabel, however, there was of course as yet no thought of getting out, but only of advancing.' The whole drive provides a compressed analogue for Isabel's venture into life so far. The blooming promising beginning, the flung fragrance (Touchett's unlooked-for bequest perhaps), then the crooked square, the preventing wall, and the enclosing courtyard—the whole passage subtly prepares us for what becomes explicit only much later when Isabel realizes that 'she had taken all the first steps in the purest confidence, and then she had suddenly found the infinite vistas of a multiplied life to be a dark, narrow alley with a dead wall at the end.' And note the geography of the following image. 'Instead of leading to the high places of happiness, from which the world could seem to lie below one, so that one could look down with a sense of exaltation and advantage, and judge and choose and pity, it led rather downward and earthward, into the realms of restriction and depression where the sound of other lives, easier and freer, was heard as from above, and where it served to deepen the

feeling of failure.' Isabel thinks Osmond lives on the heights of meditation and free appreciation, but really he dwells in the depths of
calculation and constricting appropriation. Her life seemed to lead up
to the world of ends; instead she was plunging down into the world
of means. Osmond's palace of art turns out to be 'the house of darkness, the house of dumbness, the house of suffocation.' But it was the
house she chose. James knits his imagery together in the famous
description of Isabel's reaction when Osmond proposes. She feels 'a
pang that suggested to her somehow the slipping of a fine bolt—backward, forward, she couldn't have said which.' Is she about to be released or immured? In her most testing moment she is unable to distinguish what presages liberation and expansion, and what threatens
detainment and constriction. Her radical confusion is all there in the
image.

I will not here describe the many galleries and museums and other
houses and rooms Isabel passes through, but all repay careful study.
For in this book all the architecture means something of specific importance to Isabel, as of course it must to the self seeking both freedom
and form. Pansy's convent, for instance, has all the appearance of a
prison to Isabel's clearer vision. On the other hand, some architecture
can offer consolation. For example there is a beautiful passage describing a ride she takes in Rome—'the place where people had suffered'—
some time after her discovery of the truth about Osmond. 'She had
long before taken old Rome into her confidence, for in a world of
ruins the ruin of her happiness seemed a less unnatural catastrophe.
She rested her weariness upon things that had crumbled for centuries
and yet were still upright; she dropped her secret sadness into the
silence of lonely places.' It is a most moving description of the bruised
and erring spirit absorbing strengthening reminders and consoling
clues from the marred but splendid debris of human habitations of
the past. And one of the reasons why Isabel returns to Rome at the
end, renouncing the refuge of Gardencourt which she now does appreciate as sacred, is that the self has to return to the place where it
made its most defining, if mistaken, choice. That is where the work
of re-habilitation and re-education must go on. It is where knowledge
is earned. I think this is why, in the last scene of the book, we see
Isabel running from the darkening garden of meditation back into
the well-lit house of life. But before exploring that decision I want to
discuss the significance of Ralph.

IV

Ralph is of course a recurring Jamesian figure—the subtly debarred
spectator who enjoys everything in imagination and nothing in action.

Thus Ralph has 'the imagination of loving' but has 'forbidden himself the riot of expression.' All his happiness consists of 'the sweet-tasting property of the observed thing in itself.' To appreciate the 'thing in itself' is precisely to be an inhabitant of the world of ends. Ralph is wise, he is dying: 'restricted to mere spectatorship at the game of life,' banned from participation, addicted to appreciation. A true Jamesian artist figure. Suitably, he is most often seen sitting in gardens. On one occasion in particular the contrast between 'house' and 'garden' is used to good effect. This is when Ralph tells Isabel the real truth about Osmond. She, with her theories, rejects his visions—and leaves the garden. She ends the conversation 'by turning away and walking back to the house.' But Ralph cannot follow her: it is too cold for him in the house, he is too susceptible to 'the lurking chill of the high-walled court.' It does not seem to me excessive to see Ralph as the artist-meditator, who cannot function in the house of life but who indulges his imagination and speculation in the garden. He sits; he does not act. He is content to watch and appreciate Isabel; he has no thought of dominating or manipulating her. In his own way he is also an aesthete, someone who stands back and relishes the beautiful. But where Osmond is a false aesthete, Ralph has the true artistic instincts. Osmond wants to turn Isabel into a work of art (we see her at his home 'framed in the gilded doorway' already adjusting to her status as portrait); Ralph appreciates her living qualities artistically. Osmond hates Ralph because he is 'an apostle of freedom.' But as Isabel comes to see, Ralph is more intelligent, more just, better. Not egotistic, as Osmond always is. This leads up to the deathbed scene. Isabel is back at Gardencourt, happy at least that she is no longer having to act and falsify. At Gardencourt she can be her self, her true self. And, dying, Ralph comforts her: "But love remains." He tells her she has been adored and her response is revealingly simple. "Oh my brother." In Osmond Isabel thought she recognized a soul mate. She was very wrong. At last, having suffered, she realizes who is the true image of what her self wants to be—Ralph. "Oh my brother." Having seen through the false aesthetic approach to life, she now appreciates the true artistic attitude: a vision based on love, on generosity, on respect for things in themselves, and a gift of unselfish appreciation.

In taking the measure of Osmond, Isabel has started to move towards Ralph's point of view. The great chapter, forty-two, when she takes stock, is really the beginning of her deeper knowledge and clearer vision. She is starting to read things properly, as Ralph does. And with this new access of vision, Isabel becomes less active externally and more active internally. She has started on what James later called 'the subjective adventure': the adventure of trying to understand, to sound out depths, to appreciate qualities, to transcend the importuni-

ties of the ego. By the end of the book Isabel Archer has started to
become a Jamesian artist.

Just before the end we see her in the garden at Gardencourt: this
time pensive and quiet, much closer to a knowledge of true values
than when we saw her stride so confidently on to that lawn at the
start. It is now twilight: she is sitting on a bench alone. This stance,
this setting, becomes a dominant one in James's later work—not only
in the last great story "The Bench of Desolation" but in such works
as *The Ambassadors* as well as in many stories like "Crapy Cornelia"
and "Mora Montravers." In that last story, for instance, we see the
self-effacing Traffle, excluded, estranged, sitting staring at the ap-
proaching evening with only one consolation. As the night comes
down on him he has, for company, his Jamesian mind: 'exquisite,
occult, dangerous, and sacred, to which everything ministered and
which nothing could take away.' Clearly James had a recurring vision
of a person who has somehow failed to realize him (or her) self in the
physical world, who has renounced all active participation, and who
withdraws into sedentary isolation consoling himself with the fruits
of a finer, if sadder, consciousness. Isabel, we feel, is drawing towards
her truer role as she sits in the darkening garden. But she is inter-
rupted by Caspar Goodwood, who comes to disturb her on her bench
in the garden: she cannot yet enjoy Ralph's invalid immunity from
the challenge and threat of engagement. Goodwood kisses her, and in a
curious cluster of images James implies that she is both wrecked and
then freed. Goodwood brings a possessive lightning, 'but when darkness returned she was free.' I am not fully certain of James's intention
here, but the effect is this. For a long time she has wondered if her
true fate, the true realization of her self, should not have been with
Goodwood. Now for the first time she is subjected to the full force of
his sexual claims. It is a shattering experience, but it is also a release.
She was not made to go that way. There is no going back to the simple
level of life he represents. He tries to prevent her from returning to
Rome where, as he says, she has to 'play a part' and maintain a false
'form': but it is precisely this that she must, at this stage, do. She runs
back to the house: 'there were lights in the window of the house; they
shone far across the lawn.' She reaches the door. 'Here only she paused.
She looked all about her; she listened a little; then she put her hand
on the latch. She had not known where to turn; but she knew now.
There was a very straight path.' James has annoyed readers by not
saying what that path is. But I think the wonderful suggestivity of
this last scene tells us all we need. The last pause and lingering look
surely imply that she is reluctant to leave the garden—a refuge and a
place of meditation. But she cannot opt out of her fate so easily, just

as even more she cannot return to American innocence and physical simplicity with Goodwood. She chose her room in the house of life and she must return to it. She must return to the chill and ruins of Rome: for the self cannot back out of a mistaken course but only push through and move beyond. But she takes back with her a new vision, a deeper understanding, a capacity for modest unegotistical contemplation which all promise a richer future—a future in which she will come to a true realization of what her real self is. It is beside the point to ask whether she will divorce Osmond. When she has attained her new vision, he simply shrinks into insignificance, just as Madame Merle melts away to America. We do not even hear his voice for the last seventy pages or so of the book, and by the end of the book we feel that Isabel has attained the most important kind of freedom, an internal one. She is liberated from her twisted vision and her confused values. She can see through all false appearances. She returns to Italy, to the 'ruins' she herself was partly responsible for. But she will not, we feel, ever again be subordinate to the deceptions and calculations of a worldling like Osmond. Even if she does not break out of the house and kick over the traces, and even if she never again indulges in any more passions, her future will be quite other. For her way of looking has changed. Now I think one might fairly suggest that James, in fact, could not see exactly what sort of future such a person might have, how she might take up her place again in the social scene. We can admire Isabel's fine stoicism and admit at the same time that it is hard to visualize the details of her future. And this, I think, is because James is already feeling the necessary connection between the artistic observation of life *and* the renunciation of active participation in it. As Isabel becomes more the artist, in her mind, so she will withdraw from social involvement, if not physically then at least psychologically. If she never returns to sit in the garden of Gardencourt, then we may be sure she will spend many later years reposing in the garden of her mind. With James's later artist figures or observers, the attempt at any active participation is all but abandoned from the start. Hyacinth Robinson finds no satisfying role or niche for himself in society and shoots himself. Lambert Strether develops a new complex comprehensiveness of vision and appreciation, but to retain it, it is essential that he must not get 'anything for myself'—no spoils, no physical relationships. The narrator of *The Sacred Fount* is the conscience of society, at the cost of never enjoying its actual embrace. There are other such figures, but none perhaps so humanly comprehensible as Isabel Archer, in whom we can see the erring self emerging into the incipient artist. With later characters the divorce between action and observation is almost accepted as inevitable from the start. It would seem that James, in his own way, came to share Goethe's reflection that 'the acting man is always without conscience; no one has conscience but the observing man.' If nothing else, *The Portrait of a Lady* shows us the birth of a conscience out of the spoiling of a life.

Ironic Melodrama
in *The Portrait of a Lady*

by *Manfred Mackenzie*

I

My argument in this paper is concerned primarily with *The Portrait of a Lady*, although I think its implications reach out to a good deal of Henry James's early writing. It may be put very briefly as follows: *The Portrait* is constructed from the materials of melodrama, and its intensities arise from the action of James's irony upon these materials; it might best be described as an ironic melodrama.

Before going on to discuss the novel in detail,[1] however, we need to consider separately the two terms involved in this description. Originally, of course, melodrama meant "song-drama"; it referred to a kind of entertainment devised by the early nineteenth-century French theater, which used music to support the effects of the action on stage. Being pseudo-dramatic from the start, a form of drama relying on effects which did not proceed from the characters themselves, melodrama has thus come to be associated with the wrong sort of theater, with "theater," in fact. We think of behavior in it—and even in the finer melodrama that James knew in Paris—as being assumed rather than explored, as subserving plot, which aims at evoking sensation and sentiment. Emotions in melodrama are powerful—if we could but believe in their simplified power. The characters tend to be exclusively good or exclusively bad, and they are dedicated to one another's downfall. And in the end the good escape intact since they have been threatened only in order to make the repulse of the duly indulged evil more sensational. In short, melodrama, whether naive or sophisticated, is direful sentimentality.

"Ironic Melodrama in The Portrait of a Lady*" by Manfred Mackenzie. From Modern Fiction Studies, XII (Spring, 1966), 7–23. Copyright © 1966 by Purdue University-Purdue Research Foundation. Reprinted by permission of Purdue University-Purdue Research Foundation.*

[1] *The Portrait of a Lady* (New York: Scribner's, 1908). All references are to the New York Edition.

Now it is clear that melodramatic conventions are behind much of James's fiction. One thinks of the more hectic inflammations of the marvellous in his work, of the "family secret" in *The American* and the anarchist plot of *The Princess Casamassima*. There are outcrops of Gothicism in "Gabrielle de Bergerac" and *The Turn of the Screw*, which is his superfine *Castle of Otranto*. Again and again James reverts to the figure of the *femme fatale* or, after coming under Ibsen's influence, the "strong woman." He is frequently drawn to the figure of the defenceless child—*What Maisie Knew* might be his subtly relentless *David Copperfield*. And in *The Portrait* itself we find the story of the heiress betrayed, a staple convention of melodrama with its strong element of victimization and implicit idealization of the moral attitudes assumed to be held by the audience. This story appears in *Washington Square* and *The Wings of the Dove* as well, and is a kind of simple unit that James vexes and refines in many fascinating ways.

Irony, on the other hand, is a form of analogy that proposes a congruity between things that are obviously incongruous, and then brings to our notice the obvious fact of the incongruity only to reinforce the proposed congruity by treating it as if it could not really matter. It does this, moreover, in the service of ethical norms, and is "detached" only in a very limited sense. Given this, it is obvious that the ironist will find plenty of opportunities for sport with melodrama. He abhors melodrama's reliance on moral opposites (though he needs these opposites in order to be ironic in the first place), and resists its purposes by so contriving that its opposites are not opposites at all but one and the same thing; and hence by showing either that it is more trivial than its own implicit self-estimate would make out, or, more rarely, that it is not melodrama at all but drama. We can even be persuaded of both these alternatives within the one work: in a novel like *Washington Square,* for example, melodrama is unreal (or silly) and real. But whichever the case, an irony having behind it a strong ethical faculty has corrected melodrama's simplified assumptions.

II

In *The Portrait of a Lady* the melodramatic scheme we find in *Washington Square* reappears, although it does so in a very much more complicated form. We find, too, *Washington Square*'s kind of correlation of melodrama and irony. For *The Portrait* studies a person whom we would describe as imagining and acting melodramatically when her moral life is in jeopardy. In other words, Isabel Archer's sensibility is such that she subtly turns herself into a theatrical type;

she enacts, at least in the second half of the novel, a melodrama within a melodrama.[2] In spite of the obvious differences between them, then, she is related generically to Lavinia Penniman as one of James's many theatrical women characters, and is both a melodramatic and an ironic agent. It follows that the novel, as her portrait, is melodramatic yet is not melodramatic.

The point can best be made by discussing one of the novel's special achievements, one which James himself singled out in his Preface— Isabel Archer's "extraordinary meditative vigil"[3] in Chapter XLII. It is special for two reasons perhaps. For one thing James never gets quite so much inside Isabel's consciousness either before or after this chapter; generally his tone tells us that he is standing further off than he is here. Again, this chapter is one of the earliest prolonged appearances of the psychological "picture" of the late novels, the rolling, poetic *oratio obliqua* reporting the character's rather than the author's sense of the situation. This understood, we can go on to extract some of its central metaphors:[4]

> Isabel wandered among these ugly possibilities until she had completely lost her way; some of them, as she suddenly encountered them, seemed ugly enough. Then she broke out of the labyrinth, rubbing her eyes. (II, 188)

> . . . for her soul was haunted with terrors which crowded to the foreground of thought as quickly as a place was made for them. (II, 188)

> Then the shadows had begun to gather; it was as if Osmond deliberately, almost malignantly, had put the lights out one by one. The dusk at first was vague and thin, and she could still see her way in it. But it steadily deepened, and if now and again it had occasionally lifted there were certain corners of her prospect that were impenetrably black. (II, 190)

> But she had seen only half his nature then, as one saw the disk of the moon when it was partly masked by the shadow of the earth. She saw the full moon now—she saw the whole man. (II, 191)

[2] See T. S. Eliot's "Wilkie Collins and Dickens" in *Selected Essays, 1917–32* (London, 1932), p. 415: "The principal character [of Collins's *The Haunted Hotel*], the fatal woman, is herself obsessed by the idea of fatality; her motives are melodramatic. . . . In this story, as the chief character is internally melodramatic, the story itself ceases to be merely melodramatic, and partakes of true drama." Another example of the internally melodramatic character is Giovanni in Ford's *'Tis Pity She's a Whore*. See H. J. Oliver, *The Problem of John Ford* (Melbourne, 1955), p. 95: ". . . Ford is faced with the problem of showing on the stage a character who in real life would act melodramatically. He had to give a realistic presentation of a melodramatic action: it has seemed to many a melodramatic presentation of reality. The difference in drama is very slight."

[3] *The Art of the Novel*, ed. R. P. Blackmur (New York, 1934), p. 57.

[4] This and the following passages from the New York edition show scarcely any alteration from their original serialized form.

But when . . . she had followed him further and he had led her into
the mansion of his own habitation, then, *then* she had seen where she
really was.

She could live it over again, the incredulous terror with which she had
taken the measure of her dwelling. Between those four walls she had
lived ever since; they were to surround her for the rest of her life. It
was the house of darkness, the house of dumbness, the house of suffocation. Osmond's beautiful mind gave it neither light nor air; Osmond's
beautiful mind indeed seemed to peep down from a small high window
and mock at her. (II, 196)

He took himself so seriously; it was something appalling. Under all his
culture, his cleverness, his amenity, under his good-nature, his facility, his
knowledge of life, his egotism lay hidden like a serpent in a bank of
flowers. (II, 196)

When she saw this rigid system close about her, draped though it was in
pictured tapestries, that sense of darkness and suffocation of which I
have spoken took possession of her; she seemed shut up with an odour
of mould and decay. She had resisted of course; at first very humorously,
ironically, tenderly; then, as the situation grew more serious, eagerly,
passionately, pleadingly. (II, 199)

The chapter concludes with a vision of the conspirators Isabel has
found together in Chapter XL, a vision which energizes the rest of the
novel and which has provoked her vigil in the first place:

When the clock struck four she got up; she was going to bed at last,
for the lamp had long since gone out and the candles burned down
to their sockets. But even then she stopped again in the middle of the
room and stood there gazing at a remembered vision—that of her husband and Madame Merle unconsciously and familiarly associated. (II,
205)

We might practise a little critical distortion here and imagine for a
moment this chapter set apart from its context. Ignorant of any quali-
fying ironies we should unhesitatingly regard Gilbert Osmond on what
James clearly means to be Isabel's own terms, as a Monster of Un-
mitigated Malignity; an impression which would be strengthened by
Isabel's conviction that "these shadows were not an emanation from
her own mind" (II, 190), and that she has done justice, passionate
justice, to her relation with Osmond. Correspondingly, if Isabel imagines Osmond as a Monster, then she herself must become the nominal
figure of Betrayed Innocence. In short, taking the evidence of Chapter
XLII in isolation, we should think a subtle but nonetheless dire
melodrama was being enacted.

Yet such an impression would (or should) be irreconcilable with
our sense of the novel as a whole. Isabel is not a cruelly coerced victim.
Nor is Osmond the monster that this chapter or any summary of the

plot might suggest. The one exists for us after some forty chapters as a genuine, fully complex person, while the other, though odious enough, is recognizably human. Their marriage too is every bit as much the consequence of Isabel's own will—her prized faculty of choice—as of Osmond's conspiracy. But if this is so, why does Chapter XLII look like melodrama? Why does Isabel seem to experience the same terror of Osmond as Pansy when, unlike Pansy, she is hardly an *"ingénue* in a French play"? (I, 401). Are we, indeed, to distrust Isabel's point of view here, and because she acts henceforth on these intuitions, during the rest of the novel?

Having taken Chapter XLII out of its context, we shall have to put it back in again in order to answer these puzzles. And when we do so, we come up against the familiar and difficult Jamesian process, the translation, in the mannered theater of his Europe, of a strict moral sense into an aesthetic sense, of believing into acting (acting with a strong theatrical meaning). We can see the beginnings of this process in Isabel in her rejection of Lord Warburton: "What she felt was that a territorial, a political, a social magnate had conceived the design of drawing her into the system in which he rather invidiously lived and moved. A certain instinct, not imperious, but persuasive, told her to resist—murmured to her that virtually she had a system and an orbit of her own" (I, 144). Rather than being some Gwendolen Harleth of the international scene, Isabel is an Emersonian St. Joan being coun-selled by her "voices." [5] She insists on seeing a ghost, the ghost of romantic novels, on taking part in and against "life" and "the usual chances and dangers . . . [that] most people know and suffer" (I, 187); some attainment, she believes, some spiritually aristocratic destiny that paradoxically involves her with common fates, still awaits her. Here one already sees the makings of the Heroic role she eventually discovers for herself. She begins to be at once an actor and her own producer, and, amusingly in this case, her own audience, since War-burton, a man with a sense of limitations, cannot understand her idealism.

Isabel is of course enormously encouraged in her romantic quest for a role by Ralph, who may ultimately be the novel's actual hero as well as a nominal one. Ralph lives for his "imagination of loving" (I, 54), a kind of ironic-creative adoration. He is Isabel's best audience without quite being, as he thinks, "restricted to mere spectatorship at the game of life" (I, 210). He is also her producer: " . . . her cousin amused himself with calling her 'Columbia' and accusing her of a patriotism so heated that it scorched. He drew a caricature in which she was represented as a very pretty young woman dressed, on the lines of the

[5] Hardly an "Emersonian Becky Sharp," Richard Poirier, *The Comic Sense of Henry James* (London, 1960), p. 217.

prevailing fashion, in the folds of the national banner" (I, 83). The
detail typifies Ralph's function with regard to his cousin, and elsewhere
James shows him admiring a sort of *Concert Champêtre* in which a
gentleman standing beneath a nymph on a pedestal serenades two
ladies; and later still we find him actually seated beneath such a nymph
while he discusses Isabel's engagement with her. He is a unique sort
of artist, the white magician of the realistic romance who gilds the
heroine with the half of his fortune.

Warburton is both attracted to and afraid of Isabel's imagination;
Ralph sponsors it in the hope that it will fertilize her moral life:
Osmond flatters her sense of role. "Go everywhere," he tells her, "do
everything; get everything out of life. Be happy—be triumphant"
(II, 16). Like Ralph, he is "creating" Isabel. With supremely cunning
intelligence he is putting a role, a mission, in her way just when she is
most conscious of needing one. Thus he courts her with studied self-
deprecatory talk of "marrying foreigners, forming artificial tastes,
playing tricks with our natural mission" (II, 374). And Mme. Merle
meanwhile discusses her "mission in life" (I, 398) with Mrs. Touchett.

That Isabel comes to live by a crusading impulse is nowhere more
clearly shown than in her attitude to Ralph's attack on Osmond, the
black magician of the realistic romance. As she replies, she develops
a kind of heroic momentum of which she is highly conscious:

> "I'm very just. . . . I've always believed in your wisdom," she went on,
> boasting of her quietness, yet speaking with a kind of contained exalta-
> tion. It was her passionate desire to be just . . . she went on, having
> caught a glimpse, as she thought, of the heroic line and desiring to
> advance in that direction. "I see you've some special idea; I should like
> very much to hear it. I'm sure it's disinterested; I feel that. It seems a
> strange thing to argue about, and of course I ought to tell you definitely
> that if you expect to dissuade me you may give it up. You'll not move
> me an inch; it's too late. As you say, I'm caught. Certainly it won't be
> pleasant for you to remember this, but your pain will be in your own
> thoughts. I shall never reproach you." (II, 67–68)

The grand manner rhetoric is brilliantly done. Isabel has all the air
of looking at her situation squarely and fending off an imputed evil;
she is Columbia indulging herself in a pearly robe she can't quite
afford. At the end of the scene she again turns on Ralph "a face of
elation—absolutely and perversely of gratitude. His opposition had
made her own conception of her conduct clearer to her" (II, 75). Having
tried out the role here and elsewhere, Isabel has for the moment defined
herself—she is a Heroine of romance defending the Good in an uncertain world.

Scenes like this one do a lot to prepare us for Chapter XLII, in which
we find Isabel still *acting*. But the role of Heroine she has found in the

earlier half of the novel has now given way to another, rather strained part of Wife-on-Osmond's-terms. And this second role has itself all but given way to a third and secret one, not as forty chapters of realistic romance might have led us to expect, that of Heroine campaigning for the Good so much as that of Innocence Betrayed by the very Bad, nominal Villain. In formal terms, the realistic romance has given way to ironic melodrama: "It was not her fault—she had practised no deception; she had only admired and believed. She had taken all the first steps in the purest confidence, and then she had suddenly found the infinite vista of a multiplied life to be a dark, narrow alley with a dead wall at the end" (II, 189). What we have to remember here, however, is that Isabel's Heroic and her Betrayed roles are not opposite but complementary ones, that both are assumed out of her not entirely attractive egotism. Whereas the unacknowledged impulse to free herself of the burden of her money has been behind the Heroine, behind the Innocent Betrayed is the desire to suppress the knowledge of that same, unattractive impulse. Now as ever Isabel must think well of herself: "Isabel's cheek burned when she asked herself if she had really married on a factitious theory, in order to do something finely appreciable with her money. But she was able to answer quickly enough that this was only half the story" (II, 193). (It is surely Chapter XLII that James refers to in his unequivocal authorial intrusion in Chapter XLVII: "I have mentioned how passionately she needed to feel that her unhappiness should not have come to her through her own fault" [II, 281].) Thus Isabel's reductions of her relationship with Osmond to simple, even crude, contrasts are ironically among her complexities.

All this means that Isabel creates, to a large extent anyway, the melodrama of *The Portrait of a Lady*. As both actress and her own producer, she is responsible for it. It is her feeling that makes Osmond remind us of the type from which he derives, the fortune-hunter of melodrama. In fact it might be said that Isabel, the heroine, actually victimizes Osmond, the nominal and by now ostensible villain—"Ah, what a monster you make him out!" (II, 343), Edward Rosier tells her. Victimizes, because James, and the novel as a whole, insist that Osmond is entirely credible as a person: he is described in the Notebooks as "narrow," [6] and shown in the climactic Chapter LI painting a miniature; Mrs. Touchett calls him a "curious creature" (I, 396); and in his analysis Ralph can find no more telling word for him than "small" (II, 70). By coming to imitate melodrama, then, Isabel simultaneously becomes an ironic agent after Lavinia Penniman's fashion. Her melodramatic imagination absorbs the potentially sensational content of James's plot, with the result that the novel is, yet is not, melodramatic.

[6] *The Notebooks of Henry James,* ed. F. O. Matthiessen and Kenneth B. Murdock (New York, 1955), p. 15.

Of course, to accept this reading of Isabel's characterization, and therefore of her account of Osmond, is to reject a standard reading which
describes Osmond as a "Machiavellian instrument," [7] or a "figure of
unrelieved malignity, but scarcely a believable human being," [8] or the
incarnation of "emotional cannibalism," [9] or an Iago of "absolute
malignity" whose "conquest of Isabel is intrigue in its purest form." [10]
This, it seems to me, simply accepts Isabel's construal of her situation
at its face value.

Perhaps the whole matter comes down to the ambiguity of Isabel's
"ardent good faith" (II, 74), or what I have called her crusading impulse. As we know from the case of Madame de Mauves, this is a
quality as intensely simplifying as it is attractive. We have to keep in
mind, therefore, that it is this Isabel of extravagant good faith who
judges Osmond: "It was her scorn of his assumptions, it was this that
made him draw himself up . . . that she should turn the hot light of
her disdain upon his own conception of things—this was a danger he
had not allowed for" (II, 201).

> She had spoken of his insulting her, but it suddenly seemed to her that
> this ceased to be a pain. He was going down—down; the vision of such
> a fall made her almost giddy: that was the only pain. . . .
> "Where's the letter you told me he [Warburton] had written me?" her
> husband demanded.
> "I haven't the least idea; I haven't asked him."
> "You stopped it on the way," said Osmond.
> Isabel slowly got up; standing there in her white cloak, which covered
> her to her feet, she might have represented the angel of disdain, first
> cousin to that of pity. "Oh, Gilbert, for a man who was so fine—!" she
> exclaimed in a long murmur. (II, 275–276)

After this last exchange Osmond's humiliated reply, "I was never so
fine as you," should disturb us. Whether one likes it or not, he is being
done some injustice. In the subtle dialectic of their relationship Isabel's
incandescence, which James has shown us we must criticize as well as
admire, blackens him.[11]

[7] H. R. Hays, "Henry James, the Satirist," *Hound and Horn,* VII (April–May
1934), 516.

[8] Leo B. Levy, *Versions of Melodrama: A Study of the Fiction and Drama of
Henry James, 1865–1897* (Berkeley: University of California Press, 1957), p. 46.

[9] Lyall H. Powers, *"The Portrait of a Lady:* 'The Eternal Mystery of Things,' "
Nineteenth-Century Fiction, XIV (September 1959), 149.

[10] J. A. Ward, *The Imagination of Disaster: Evil in the Fiction of Henry James*
(Lincoln: University of Nebraska Press, 1961), pp. 51, 129.

[11] It is worth noting that James's probable model, *Middlemarch,* dramatizes the
same kind of dialectic in Dorothea's relationship with Mr. Casaubon. George
Eliot's dialectic is more openly presented, of course, and we don't need to allow
for any theatrical central intelligence such as Isabel's. Another difference is that

III

We can move on now to the dramatic consequences of Chapter XLII. *The Portrait* has given Isabel two grand entrances, at Gardencourt where she is so felicitously studious of being Columbia-Diana; and into the "Europe" or Experience of the novel, Rome, where she just as studiously represents Osmond—a fine lady whose "light step drew a mass of drapery behind it . . . [whose] intelligent head sustained a majesty of ornament" (II, 143). She is first a would-be romance Heroine and then, simultaneously, Wife-on-Osmond's-terms and Innocence Betrayed. The action that now follows on this second entrance James devotes to resolving the considerable tensions between these roles of Isabel's by finding her a fourth one.

Let us look at Isabel's representation of Osmond, her producer by this time rather than her audience. In spite of her knowledge of Pansy's affection for Rosier, she is persuaded by Mme. Merle to use her influence with Warburton as regards the girl: she wants to please her husband, and this is her occasion. She sees Osmond about the matter, cannot help humiliating him about it, but tacitly agrees a second time to assist (Chapter XLI). She is made partly aware of Warburton's equivocal motives in the dance scene in Chapter XLIII, and fully aware of them in Chapter XLV by a dangerously probing Ralph; yet she still suppresses her knowledge of Pansy's affection in favor of Mme. Merle's and Osmond's plan. The scene that follows her interview with Ralph brings this public part to a climax. Trying to persuade Pansy to her husband's view, Isabel finds herself forced into hideous insincerities: her moral and aesthetic senses are discordant. It now occurs to her suddenly that, "It was what she was doing for Osmond; it was what one had to do for Osmond!" (II, 257). But these, surely, are the lines of Isabel's other part, the private part of Chapter XLII, according to which she refuses to recognize her own fault. Isabel may be a Wife-on-Osmond's-terms; she is really Innocence Betrayed.

Pansy in an exquisite way eases Isabel out of her ugly position. So does the plot, for Warburton soon announces his departure. Isabel has now almost exhausted the role for which she has been miscast without yet finding public vent for the other, secret one into which she puts her heart. As he leaves, however, Warburton actually presents her with her occasion (while James embarrasses her with a sharp irony). He tells Pansy in front of Isabel that she has a guardian angel, a compliment

Dorothea transcends this dialectic by coming eventually to pity her husband, while Isabel simply intensifies her situation. For a different view of the two dramas, see George Levine, "Isabel, Gwendolen, and Dorothea," *ELH,* XXX (September 1963), 248–251.

which Pansy is glad to confirm. Here is a new role, one that revives Isabel's old sense of being a Heroine and that absorbs her new conception of herself as Innocence Betrayed. She can drop her exhausted role of Wife-on-Osmond's-terms and find another mission—she will protect Pansy, the ideal *jeune fille* whom she herself has wronged, while nourishing herself on her own aggrieved feelings. This exchange James confirms during the rest of the chapter. Warburton goes, and there follows a scene between Isabel and the thwarted Osmond in which Isabel, who in the previous chapter has done her best for Osmond to the point of betraying Pansy, now defends Pansy against her father.

After this (Chapter XLVI), we find a very close identification of Isabel with Pansy—long prepared for, it is one of the novel's most brilliant developments, and it needs more attention than it usually gets. As Isabel noticed when they first met in Chapter XXVI, Pansy is "an *ingénue* in a French play . . . a sheet of blank paper—the ideal *jeune fille* of foreign fiction" (I, 401). But by Chapter XL she has begun to feel the pressure of the girl's "ardent coercive faith" (Isabel, we remember, has her own "ardent good faith"): "On her own side her sense of the girl's dependence was more than a pleasure; it operated as a definite reason when motives threatened to fail her. She had said to herself that we must take our duty where we find it, and that we must look for it as much as possible. Pansy's sympathy was a direct admonition; it seemed to say that here was an opportunity, not eminent perhaps, but unmistakable. Yet an opportunity for what Isabel could hardly have said; in general, to be more for the child than the child was able to be for herself" (II, 161). Isabel is not yet quite living for Innocence. However, by Chapter XLIII she has come further to identify herself with Pansy's (through Edward Rosier's) fortunes: "But she suddenly felt touched; her own unhappiness, after all, had something in common with his [Rosier's], and it came over her, more than before, that here, in recognisable, if not in romantic form, was the most affecting thing in the world—young love struggling with adversity" (II, 208). And by Chapter L her self-identification with the girl she has once thought limited is unreserved, even overwrought. Osmond announces that Pansy is returning to the convent until, he implies, she learns to obey him: "The old Protestant tradition had never faded from Isabel's imagination, and as her thoughts attached themselves to this striking example of her husband's genius—she sat looking, like him, at the basket of flowers—poor little Pansy became the heroine of a tragedy" (II, 349). Isabel has come far from her original perception of Pansy as the *ingénue,* the ideal *jeune fille* of foreign melodramas. To her sense, Pansy's fate is to a large extent her own, a "tragic" one. Pansy is an Innocent Betrayed, too.

It will have become partially clear by now that a good deal of the action in the second half of the novel derives from melodrama, that, in fact, it copies the main action in little. The convention behind the main plot pits the good against the evil for possession of the innocent protagonist, and threatens good only to let it triumph sensationally at the last; there are on the one hand those who have Isabel's welfare at heart, Goodwood, Warburton and the Touchetts, and on the other, Mme. Merle, Osmond, and to some extent the Countess Gemini. In the subplot involving Pansy, however, Isabel, the nominal victim of the larger melodrama, is in relation to Pansy as Ralph has been to herself just before her marriage, and as Warburton and Goodwood are to her on their visits after her marriage; she is now a Heroine where they have been the composite, nominal Hero. Edward Rosier is joined with her in this function; as a connoisseur who will give up all for love, he provides an interesting likeness to Ralph. Warburton provides yet another link with the main action. His equivocal attentions to Pansy help to enforce the identification that James wants between Isabel and the girl, at the same time that they keep Isabel as the center of interest. In short, we have a second, "little" melodrama within a melodrama: we are to set the Isabel (Warburton: Rosier)—Pansy—Osmond: Mme. Merle relationship over against the Ralph: Goodwood: Warburton—Isabel—Osmond: Mme. Merle relationship.

Naturally, this melodrama in little is meant primarily to exhibit Isabel. To some extent it objectifies and intensifies her role as she likes to conceive of it in Chapter XLII. Like Pansy, she is another Innocence Betrayed. On the other hand, the moment Isabel is compared with Pansy, it becomes obvious that she is Innocence Betrayed only in a limited sense—that she is naturally too powerful a person to suit the role. In fact, the comparison shows us that she has if anything reverted to her first role of romance Heroine (Heroine, now campaigning for an actual Innocence Betrayed rather than a vague Good). Thus the melodramatic subplot has an ironic function. It modifies our sense of Isabel by showing her strong and helpless at the same time.

That Isabel is alternately helpless and strong in her relationships James shows in the two chapters given to the novel's first climax, LI and LII. Having come in the first of these to tell Osmond that she must go to see the dying Ralph, she vilifies him characteristically—"It's your own opposition that's calculated. It's malignant" (II, 354)—and he replies:

"I think we should accept the consequences of our actions, and what I value most in life is the honour of a thing!"

He spoke gravely and almost gently; the accent of sarcasm had dropped out of his tone. It had a gravity which checked his wife's quick emotion; the resolution with which she had entered the room found itself caught in a mesh of fine threads. His last words were not a command, they constituted a kind of appeal; and, though she felt that any expression of respect on his part could only be a refinement of egotism, they represented something transcendent and absolute, like the sign of the cross or the flag of one's country. He spoke in the name of something sacred and precious—the observance of a magnificent form. (II, 356)

One notices here Osmond's deference to Isabel's right to choose, the right she has always prized most. In a sort of half-sincere, half-cunning manner, he waves a banner in the name of what she has chosen; and the moral crusader who has been all resolution is stunned, transformed as ever by the "magical" blight of her husband's touch: "Her faculties, her energy, her passion, were all dispersed again; she felt as if a cold, dark mist had suddenly encompassed her" (II, 358). Having lost all impetus, she does not recover until the Countess Gemini reveals all in the next scene—the scene, by the way, in which the novel most closely approaches straight melodrama. Isabel now seems to be aroused to a numb compassion, apparently for Ralph, a compassion which strengthens noticeably in her final interview with Pansy in the following chapter. Like herself, Isabel sees, Pansy has been vanquished—"she had seen the reality" (II, 385)—by Mme. Merle and Osmond; and she promises not to desert this other very real and pathetic Innocence Betrayed. James tells us they are like sisters, but clearly the scene is meant to assert Isabel's role as strong guardian angel just as much as this identification. She is not, at the same time that she is, an Innocent Betrayed—a creative irony we should not miss.

So far I have tried to show how James conveys in these darker sections Isabel's self-idealization and corresponding, subtle vilification of Osmond. *The Portrait* now confronts us with the problem of her leaving and then deciding to return to the husband she vilifies, a decision making most sense, I think, as the resolution of the various roles she has found herself playing. In the first place, going to Gardencourt against Osmond's wishes amounts to her finally abandoning her uncomfortable part of Wife-on-his-terms. Gardencourt, moreover, further strengthens the Heroine in Isabel—something that her association with Pansy has already revived—since it is the stage of her debut in the role. But even while she sees herself come full circle, she is aware of a change. Experience is no longer a theoretical matter of seeing a ghost, but the matter of her marriage. Indeed Experience has betrayed "Innocence," and made of her an Innocence Betrayed. Therefore, unable to deny either of her two remaining roles, she returns to Osmond as a refreshed Heroine campaigning for Innocence Betrayed—the ironic, "come true" version of the active romance mission she has wanted from the start. She reenters the state of Experience (which is something that can only be said of a romance heroine) crusading willingly for her girlish idealism, as Isabel *vindex,* as another Madame de Mauves.

On this view, Isabel's association with Pansy comes to be properly fulfilled. It is less than it has seemed James's ruse in lieu of something better, since Pansy's cause is his heroine's "objective correlative," a second chance to carry the "Innocence" of her own Gardencourt life into Experience. Indeed, Pansy allows Isabel's moral and aesthetic senses to harmonize at last: if the girl is the ostensible Innocence Betrayed (Isabel herself is this figure nominally) in her projected melodrama with a Gothic tinge, she will be the ostensible Heroine pitted on behalf of Innocence Betrayed against the malignant castellan of Palazzo Roccanera.

We can hypothesize that Isabel reenters Experience as a crusader partly because no evidence offers itself in James's somewhat truncated conclusion to suggest that she has changed her view of herself as wronged but not wronging. It has been said of the wonderful scene at Ralph's deathbed that, "At last, and for the only time in the novel, two people speak to one another without a semblance of theatricality or shame or self-elevation." [12] But there is, one fears, fiction even in this apparently unadorned moment. Both characters have dropped all play, but neither is fundamentally altered: "for nothing mattered now but the only knowledge that was not pure anguish—the knowledge that they were looking at the truth together. 'He married me for the money,' she said. She wished to say everything; she was afraid he might die before she had done so" (II, 414–415). Isabel's "everything"— James is surely ironic here—includes the acknowledgment that Osmond has been genuinely in love with her, but still does not include that aspect of the situation which she has dismissed in Chapter XLII: "For this was the fantastic fact. At bottom her money had been a burden, had been on her mind, which was filled with the desire to transfer the weight of it to some other conscience, to some more prepared receptacle. . . . Isabel's cheek burned when she asked herself if she had really married on a factitious theory, in order to do something finely appreciable with her money. But she was able to answer quickly enough that this was only half the story" (II, 193). Although, of course, Osmond is more culpable in this, both he and Isabel have married for the money. If Ralph has acted disinterestedly in respect to it, their egotism has focussed in it. But Isabel will not recognize her fault. Morally inviolate, as she believes, she sees only Osmond's.

The final scene with Goodwood has often been vaguely called melodramatic when, in fact, it is a stroke of profoundly ironic melodrama. James has tested Isabel throughout with her suitors, having her meet them several times while in quest of a role before her marriage, and again after her marriage. Finally, when she gains apparent freedom from Osmond, James tests her yet again even at the risk of clumsiness,

[12] Poirier, p. 242.

and Ralph, Warburton, and Goodwood all appear with their appeals. Of these the last is of special interest. Goodwood has seen Osmond in his Gothic fortress and judged the situation for himself, and he now tells Isabel with passion: "You're the most unhappy of women, and your husband's the deadliest of fiends. . . . How can you pretend you're not heart-broken? You don't know what to do—you don't know where to turn. It's too late to play a part; didn't you leave all that behind you in Rome? . . . When I know such a horror as that, how can I keep myself from wishing to save you?" (II, 432–433). But while Goodwood has to some extent judged correctly, he has not reckoned on Isabel's recent development, on the resurgence of her natural strength. In his passion, he mistakes her role; and she is now shocked out of her numbness into her crusade as Heroine, thus supplanting Goodwood as the self-styled nominal Hero rescuing what he thinks is only Innocence Betrayed from the Deadliest of Fiends. His appeal comes close, but falls short. Here is the scene's melodramatic power, and its powerful irony.

The Portrait's resonant ending, one supposes, augurs a Pyrrhic victory for its heroine: she will have lost almost all chance of any obvious happiness, yet she will have the hidden pleasure of her righteousness. If this theme is latent in the conclusion, then the novel is simply consistent with James's other variations on it—*The American, What Maisie Knew, The Wings of the Dove,* perhaps *The Spoils of Poynton* and *The Golden Bowl.* In *The Wings of the Dove,* which also uses the plot discussed above, it even seems that James's religious humanism leads him to a metaphysical statement of it: here (and in *Little Dorrit*) Victorian melodrama reaches its apotheosis as semi-allegory. Indeed, apart from its suiting the theme of American innocence and European experience, this may ultimately be the reason for James's interest in the formula-plot we find in *The Portrait*—insisting on the triumph of innocence, and yet provoking the imagination of disaster, it offers an excellent vehicle for the theme of the Pyrrhic, or ironic, victory of innocence.

Two Problems
in *The Portrait of a Lady*

by Dorothea Krook

I. Why does Isabel go back to Osmond?

This problem has, I believe, been somewhat artificially created for modern critics by a failure in critical perspective which arises from the disposition to ignore or minimize the context, historical and dramatic, in which Isabel Archer's final decision is made. I have heard it seriously argued that Isabel "could after all have done something else"— walked out into freedom (like Nora in *A Doll's House,* presumably), or gone in for charitable works (like Dorothea Brooke in *Middlemarch*), or even perhaps taken a degree and become a pioneer in women's education, or whatever. The short answer to these bracing proposals is that Isabel Archer could have done none of these things. Her circumstances, historical, psychological, and dramatic—in particular the dramatic—absolutely proscribe any "end" to her life other than marriage, and any duties, responsibilities or even serious interests other than those belonging to or arising out of that estate. This is part of James's *donnée* in the story; and to intrude other, extrinsic possibilities—or, rather, pseudo-possibilities—is to fall into a vicious abstractionism that is fatal to literary criticism.

This is the failure in critical perspective at its most elementary level. At a less elementary level, it springs from a preconception almost as intrusive and misleading as the other—namely, a disposition to take too emancipated a view of the marriage-bond and the "naturalness" of divorce. Why did not Isabel divorce Osmond? is now the question; and the answer is that what we are shown of Isabel Archer's nature and of her view of marriage (as distinct from her modern critics') makes it

"Two Problems *in* The Portrait of a Lady." *From* The Ordeal of Consciousness *in* Henry James *by Dorothea Krook (New York: Cambridge University Press, 1962), pp. 357–69. Copyright © 1962 by Cambridge University Press. Reprinted by permission of the publisher. Quotations from* The Portrait of a Lady *are from the New York Edition of* The Novels and Tales of Henry James, *Vols. III and IV (New York: Charles Scribner's Sons, 1908).*

abundantly clear that divorce would be for her the least natural form
of deliverance from her predicament. Leaving aside the special motive
for going back to Osmond provided by Pansy and Pansy's need of her,
which is explicitly emphasized, we are expected to remember that
loyalty or "devotion" was a conspicuous element of Isabel Archer's
nature. Gilbert Osmond, we remember, had recognized it from the
beginning: "I like her very much," he had said to Madame Merle,
"She's all you described her, and into the bargain capable, I feel, of
great devotion." In Isabel's midnight vigil we have this confirmed in
a particularly decisive (and moving) way when, reflecting on Osmond's
hatred of her "ideas," she calls her soul to witness that "she had no
opinions . . . that she would not have been eager to sacrifice in the
satisfaction of feeling herself loved for it"; and this devotion or loyalty
may be seen as a function of the moral consistency that springs so naturally, it seems, from her moral seriousness.

Her view of the marriage bond as in the highest degree solemn and
serious is closely linked with it. Marriage for her is a complete commitment of one person to another, and as such not to be set aside
even from the gravest causes; and though there is, of course, no suggestion of a Christian-theological sanction in the strict sense, it would
nevertheless be true to say that Isabel Archer takes a "sacramental"
view of marriage, as a "sanctified" union which is to be regarded as
substantially indissoluble. In the earlier parts of the story, this is implicit in the exalted view she takes of her marriage to Osmond, and her
faith in all that this most intimate of bonds can yield for the exercise
of virtue as well as for personal happiness; in the later parts, it is several times explicitly mentioned as a prime reason for her reluctance
to leave, or even to defy, her husband. Long before the end of the
story, when her cousin Ralph Touchett is lying sick in his hotel in
Rome, we learn that she is filled with "shame" and "dread" at the
thought of deliberately flouting Osmond's wishes by going to see him:

> She had not as yet undertaken to act in direct opposition to his wishes;
> he was her appointed and inscribed master; she gazed at moments with
> a sort of incredulous blankness at this fact. It weighed upon her imagina-
> tion, however; constantly present to her mind were all the traditionary
> decencies and sanctities of marriage. The idea of violating them filled
> her with shame as well as with dread, for on giving herself away she
> had lost sight of this contingency in the perfect belief that her husband's
> intentions were as generous as her own. She seemed to see, none the
> less, the rapid approach of the day when she should have to take back
> something she had solemnly bestown. Such a ceremony would be odious
> and monstrous; she tried to shut her eyes to it meanwhile.

She cannot indeed for long shut her eyes to it; for the crisis is precipi-
tated soon after this when Osmond virtually forbids her to go to

Ralph, now dying at Gardencourt. But though she does in the end defy him and go, she still, we learn, finds the ceremony "odious" and "monstrous." She has gone to her room after the scene with Osmond:

> It seemed to her that only now she fully measured the great undertaking of matrimony. Marriage meant that in such a case as this, when one had to choose, one chose as a matter of course for one's husband. "I'm afraid—yes, I'm afraid," she said to herself more than once, stopping short in her walk. But what she was afraid of was not her husband—his displeasure, his hatred, his revenge; it was not even her own later judgement of her conduct—a consideration which had often held her in check; it was simply the violence there would be in going when Osmond wished her to remain. A gulf of difference had opened between them, but nevertheless it was his desire that she should stay, it was a horror to him that she should go. She knew the nervous fineness with which he could feel an objection. What he thought of her she knew, what he was capable of saying to her she had felt; yet they were married, for all that, and marriage meant that a woman should cleave to the man with whom, uttering tremendous vows, she had stood at the altar.

Isabel's deepest and most decisive reason, however, for going back to Osmond is to be inferred from those passages in her midnight vigil in which she comes to her painful self-knowledge, in particular the knowledge of the degree in which she herself has been responsible for Osmond's self-deception about her, and the extent therefore to which she has contributed to the failure of their marriage. ("She had made herself small, pretending there was less of her than there really was . . ."; "Yes, she *had* been hypocritical; she had liked him so much," and so on.) What she comes to feel is that, having this degree of moral responsibility, she must accept the consequences; and this means going back to Osmond and enduring, simply *enduring,* her life with him as the only expiation open to her. She never, of course, puts it to herself so explicitly; but she comes as near as she can to seeing it (and saying it) in a brief passage in her last reflections at Gardencourt, when she recognizes once again that "certain obligations were involved in the very fact of marriage, and were quite independent of the quantity of enjoyment extracted from it"—and then acts on that insight.

The most explicit statement of this final position, however, comes from Osmond himself, in the bitter exchange between them when he forbids her to go to Ralph at Gardencourt; and it is like a last turn of the screw that she should have to take her most compelling reason for continuing in her wretched condition from the man who is its principal cause. The passage, though long, is worth quoting in full because, besides giving us the poignancy of Isabel's situation, it also throws a last vivid light on Osmond's view of it, and shows us how the strange *sincerity* that lurks in his care for appearances has, more than anything, the power to break down Isabel's resistance. Osmond is speaking:

> "I've never liked him [Ralph] and he has never liked me. That's why you like him—because he hates me," said Osmond with a quick, barely audible tremor in his voice. "I've an ideal of what my wife should do and should not do. She should not travel across Europe alone, in defiance of my deepest desire, to sit at the bedside of other men. Your cousin's nothing to you; he's nothing to us. You smile most expressively when I talk about *us,* but I assure you that *we, we,* Mrs. Osmond, is all I know. I take our marriage seriously; you appear to have found a way of not doing so. I'm not aware that we're divorced or separated; for me we're indissolubly united. You are nearer to me than any human creature, and I'm nearer to you. It may be a disagreeable proximity; it's one, at any rate, of our own deliberate making. You don't like to be reminded of that, I know; but I'm perfectly willing because—because—" And he paused a moment, looking as if he had something to say which would be very much to the point. "Because I think we should accept the consequences of our actions, and what I value most in life is the honour of a thing!"

Upon this speech follows the comment:

> He spoke gravely and almost gently; the accent of sarcasm had dropped out of his tone. It had a gravity which checked his wife's quick emotion; the resolution with which she had entered the room found itself caught in a mesh of fine threads. His last words were not a command, they constituted a kind of appeal; and, though she felt that any expression of respect on his part could only be a refinement of egotism, they represented something transcendent and absolute, like the sign of the cross or the flag of one's country. He spoke in the name of something sacred and precious—the observance of a magnificent form. . . . Isabel had not changed; her old passion for justice still abode within her; and now, in the very thick of her sense of her husband's blasphemous sophistry, it began to throb to a tune which for a moment promised him the victory. It came over her that in his wish to preserve appearances he was after all sincere, and that this, as far as it went, was a merit. Ten minutes before she had felt all the joy of irreflective action—a joy to which she had for so long been a stranger; but action had been suddenly changed to slow renunciation, transformed by the blight of Osmond's touch.

Isabel does go to Ralph, and to that extent does temporarily resist the blight of Osmond's touch. But his words, she presently discovers, have struck a deeper response in her than she knew at the time. What she finds in the end is that though she repudiates his reasons as blasphemous sophistry, the fact he insists on commands her most inward assent; and it is the fact that finally compels her to go back to him in despite of the reasons.

II. The Sexual Theme

To speak of James's "treatment" of the sexual theme in *The Portrait of a Lady* would be virtually meaningless, but for the striking episode between Isabel and Caspar Goodwood in the very last pages of the book. Apart from the hint about the "male" quality in Caspar Goodwood that troubles Isabel from the beginning, there is, or seems to be, until this episode no reference to it either explicit or implicit; and if the sexual theme in *The Portrait of a Lady* were indeed to rest entirely on this episode it would seem hardly worth examining. This, however, is only apparently the case. The last encounter between Isabel and Caspar Goodwood is not only peculiarly significant in itself but also illuminates previous, less conspicuous, episodes bearing on the sexual theme; and by tracing these connections one can, I believe, arrive at a reasonably complete view of James's treatment of this theme in *The Portrait of a Lady*.

The fact that in this last vivid scene Isabel should again and finally turn down Caspar Goodwood raises by itself no problem. As he kisses her, "it was extraordinarily as if, while she took it, she felt each thing in his hard manhood that had least pleased her, each aggressive fact of his face, his figure, his presence, justified of its intense identity and made one with this act of possession"; and what this means is that Goodwood will no more "do" now than he would have "done" before she married Osmond. For he is still, in a word, too crude; and the fact that Osmond's refinement has turned out to be terrible delusion does not make Goodwood's lack of it any more acceptable. In this I think, we are meant to see a last proof of Isabel's ultimate integrity. Even in her misery and despair at the prospect of resuming her life with Osmond, her judgment in this vital connection remains unimpaired: she knows that she ought not to give herself to Caspar Goodwood now any more than she ought to have given herself to Gilbert Osmond then; and this perhaps is part of what she has learnt from her disastrous mistake with Osmond.

What does raise a problem, however, is the kind and quality of the fear that Isabel appears to experience in this climactic episode. This is powerfully evoked by the sea-image (more than sufficiently "Freudian") which expresses it here. As Goodwood ends his passionate speech, she feels herself "floating" upon a sea in an ecstasy of incipient surrender:

> The world . . . had never seemed so large; it seemed to open out, all round her, to take the form of a mighty sea, where she floated in fathomless waters. She had wanted help, and here was help; it had come in a rushing torrent. . . . She believed just then that to let him take her in

his arms would be the next best thing to her dying. This belief, for a
moment, was a kind of rapture, in which she felt herself sink and sink.
In the movement she seemed to beat with her feet, in order to catch
herself, to feel something to rest on.

Then he speaks again, in a voice "harsh and terrible," and her sensation now is that of sinking: "The confusion, the noise of waters, all
the rest of it were in her . . . swimming head"; and as he kisses her
("His kiss was like white lightning, a flash that spread, and spread
again, and stayed") and she is seized with her final revulsion; this is succeeded by a sensation of drowning: "So she had heard of those wrecked
and under water following a train of images before they sink." The
next moment the "darkness" returns (after the flash of white lightning), and through it she speeds to "freedom"—away from Caspar
Goodwood, back to the house, and ultimately to Rome and Gilbert
Osmond.

In a way unusual in James's works, the image here is left to express
the whole meaning; there is none of the help so often provided by
somebody's analytical comment or interior monologue; and this is
significant not because the help is in fact needed but because it suggests on James's part a deliberate intention to leave as open as possible
the question of the "rightness" or "wrongness" of Isabel's action. She
is afraid—that is clear enough; but is she *right* to be afraid? Is she right
in particular in view of what she herself has just a moment before
recognized, "that she had never been loved before"? This sensation,
too, is conveyed by an image as violent as the white-lightning image
of the kiss. Goodwood has ended his first speech with the question,
"Why should you go back—why should you go through that ghastly
form?"; to which she answers,

> "To get away from *you!*" . . . But this expressed only a little of what
> she felt. The rest was that she had never been loved before. She had
> believed it, but this was different; this was the hot wind of the desert,
> at the approach of which the others dropped dead, like mere sweet airs
> of the garden. It wrapped her about; it lifted her off her feet, while the
> very taste of it, as of something potent, acrid and strange, forced open
> her set teeth.

So Isabel Archer knows she is being for the first time "loved"; yet
she resists it fiercely (it "forced open her set teeth"), and finally flees
from the love, the lover, indeed from the knowledge itself. What frightens and repels her is plain enough. It is the sheer violence of it—"the
hot wind of the desert"; and this fear and distaste in Isabel of the element of violence in the passion of love has (we now remember) already shown itself before this. There is, for instance, a significant passage in the early scene of Lord Warburton's proposal in the garden

at Gardencourt, to which we are sent back by the reference here to the "mere sweet airs of the garden" which drop dead before the "hot wind of the desert." Warburton has told her he is "a very judicious animal" and does not "go off easily," but when he does it's for life:

> "It's for life, Miss Archer, it's for life," Lord Warburton repeated in the kindest, tenderest, pleasantest voice Isabel had ever heard, and looking at her with eyes *charged with the light of a passion that had sifted itself clear of the baser parts of emotion—the heat, the violence, the unreason —and that burned as steadily as a lamp in a windless place.**

Again, in an earlier passage, when Isabel dismisses Lord Warburton with seeming coldness, we are told explicitly that "her coldness was not the calculation of her effect. It came from a certain fear"; and when, much later, she has a strenuous encounter with Caspar Goodwood in Florence and bursts into tears "five minutes after he had gone," the main reason for the tears is again, we may suppose, "a certain fear."

If from these episodes we may legitimately infer that Isabel Archer has a fear of sexual passion, particularly in its more "violent" aspect, two questions arise: first, to what extent is this fear "culpable" in Isabel; second, how conscious was James himself of its presence in his portrait of his engaging young woman, and if he was conscious of it, what view did he mean us to take of it?

That a young woman of Isabel Archer's sensibilities should, in that time and place in particular, feel a fear of the sexual need cause no surprise. Its mystery and terror is something that not only the young and immature experience; and only the most doctrinaire of modern theorists would want to dispute the naturalness of the fear, and to that extent also its "rightness," in someone like Isabel. This, however, seems not to be the whole explanation. The rest has to do with what we feel in Isabel as a tendency to *withdraw*—a tendency to withhold herself, to refuse to surrender herself to the relationship as a whole and *a fortiori* to its sexual demands. She herself appears to recognize this, or something like it, when she asks herself at the end of one of her agitating encounters with Lord Warburton "if she were not a cold, hard, priggish person" to find herself so unable to accept a man of such splendid parts; and the question for us is whether this seeming coldness and hardness are due to what would nowadays be called sexual frigidity, or, if they are not due to this, what their cause in fact is.

I believe it has nothing to do with frigidity, either in intention or effect, and has everything to do with that aspect of Isabel's nature already touched on which James himself saw as the center of interest in his engaging young woman. When a young woman is so constituted as to have, besides an enquiring mind and an independent spirit, an

*My emphasis.

unquenchable passion for knowledge derived from direct, first-hand experience, the most serious threat to such aspirations, especially in an earlier age than the present, is that constituted by marriage and the completeness of the surrender it involves—for someone at any rate who, like Isabel Archer, takes this absolute view of the marriage bond. With the "right person," as we say, there is of course no problem; and Isabel, we saw, joyfully embraced the opportunity to surrender herself to the right person when she thought she had found him in Gilbert Osmond. But the right person, never to be had for the wanting, was particularly not to be had for the wanting in the circle to which Isabel Archer's life was confined; her story amply confirms this—indeed is intended to exhibit this among other unalterable facts of her condition; and so long as there *is* a doubt that the person in question (Lord Warburton, Caspar Goodwood) is "right," a young woman like Isabel Archer cannot be careful enough. The seeming coldness and hardness are accordingly to be seen as self-protective indeed; but the end for which the self is being protected is (James wishes us to see) in the highest degree noble and worthwhile, and as such invites not censure but compassion for the means—the "coldness" and the "hardness," and the fear from which they spring—to which Isabel must have recourse in order to safeguard that precious end.

This, I believe, is James's principal intention in emphasizing his heroine's "fear" at certain crucial moments in the story; and it is again characteristic of James's mastery of the psychological and dramatic verisimilitudes of these moments that Isabel herself should in each instance appear puzzled and confused about its meaning, and disposed therefore to put the least creditable interpretation on her own reactions. The problem that remains turns upon Isabel's revulsion from the "violence" of the sexual passion itself, which is so clearly apparent in the final episode with Caspar Goodwood but (I suggested) is hinted at before. On the explanation I have proposed of Isabel's fear in general, it would presumably be justified on the ground that it is intrinsically incompatible with all that is *civilized* in the ideal that Isabel aspires to realize in her life. In that case, it would seem that the element of violence in sexual passion is being equated with the uncivilized or anti-civilized; and in the passages cited this indeed appears to be Isabel's attitude. In so far as it is only Isabel's attitude, there can of course be no quarrel with it. But in so far as it may also be James's own attitude, it is a cause if not for quarrel at least for further enquiry. For (as James himself is to show in some of the most important of his later works) the "violent" element—the importunate, the wanting and desiring, jealous and possessive element—in sexual passion, so far from being incompatible with the perfection of civilized virtue, is in fact (as James is to show in *The Golden Bowl* in particular), the necessary condition of this, as of all, virtue; and the question is whether James when he wrote *The Portrait of a Lady* knew what he later came to know, or whether he knew at this time as little as his heroine and consequently identified himself with her on this vital matter.

The internal evidences of the text suggest that the latter was the case—that James shared his heroine's fear of, and even revulsion from, the sexual passion in its more violent, importunate forms, and for reasons *mutatis mutandis* essentially similar to hers.* He, too, at this stage of his life felt it as a threat to the two things, one "public," the other "private" or personal, that were most precious to him—his ideal of civilization on the one side, his aspiration to dedicate his life to the practice of his art on the other. Both ends, it would have seemed to him, were better—that is, more safely—served by a passion that (in Isabel's phrase) "had sifted itself clear of the baser parts of emotion— the heat, the violence, the unreason—and that burned as steadily as a lamp in a windless place"; and both (so again it would have seemed to him) were in mortal danger when exposed to "the hot wind of the desert" which Isabel experiences in the last scene of the book.

The *prima facie* reasonableness of this view is obvious, and has in any case been argued fully and eloquently enough by James himself in the group of stories—*The Lesson of the Master* and the rest—deal- ing with the life of the artist and the insoluble problems created for him by the involvements of marriage. (The sexual theme as such, it is

---

*The main external evidences to support this view are to be found in the curious letters, recently made available by Mr. Leon Edel (in *Selected Letters of Henry James,* London: 1956), that James wrote to his family about the beloved cousin Minny Temple immediately after her death (*op. cit.,* pp. 60–64). Though they are sincere enough, and often beautiful and moving, they seem nevertheless to be tainted with a degree of detachment of the wrong kind—a holding back, an ultimate re- fusal to be really deeply and painfully involved in the life of the suffering girl, a refusal in fact to share her suffering—which brings back (with all the necessary qualifications) Isabel Archer's phrase about herself as "cold, hard and priggish." "To have known her is certainly an immense gain," he writes to his mother on 26th March 1870, "but who would have wished her to live longer on such a footing —*unless he had felt within him (what I felt little enough!) some irresistible mission to reconcile her to a world to which she was essentially hostile.* There is absolute balm in the thought of poor Minny and *rest*—rest and immortal absence!" (*Op. cit.* p. 61. My emphasis.) The "irresistible mission" James speaks of needed nothing more abstruse than love to inspire and sustain it; and what he is saying here is that he adored and admired Minny Temple but did not love her. If the suggestion, frequently made, that Isabel Archer is one of James's renderings of Minny Temple is correct, it would be confirmed by the connection between James's own imperfect capacity for love at this period of his life and the similar defect in his heroine Isabel Archer; and if, as everyone believes, Milly Theale in *The Wings of the Dove* is James's final rendering of this cousin whose life and death appear always to have haunted him, it could be argued with this same connection in mind that James's object there is not only commemorative but also expiatory.

true, is not mentioned in these stories; but readers of the story *John Delavoy* will have no difficulty in discerning the reason for this.) What is interesting to the student of Henry James's development as man and artist is that he came in time to change his view. His life's experience, it seems, contrived to teach him what he appears not to have known at the time he wrote *The Portrait of a Lady*—that passion, with all its dangers, is the sacred fount of all creative endeavor, and that to deny or sacrifice it in the name of any ideal, however noble, is a delusion which succeeds only in defeating the noble end for which the denial or sacrifice was made. *The Beast in the Jungle* is, I believe, Henry James's most poignant testimony to this hardest, most painful lesson of his life; and having learnt it, he characteristically redeems his tragic error in the most important works of his late period—*The Sacred Fount* to begin with, followed by *The Ambassadors, The Wings of the Dove,* and *The Golden Bowl*—in which the power of sexual passion to redeem (as well as destroy) is exhibited with a fullness of knowledge to be found nowhere else in the English novel.

F. O. *Matthiessen:* Free Will and Determinism

In both the original and the revision Isabel lays the most scrupulous emphasis upon the sacredness of a promise. Despite all her eagerness for culture, hers is no speculative spirit. Osmond comes to despise her for having "the moral horizon" of a Unitarian minister—"poor Isabel, who had never been able to understand Unitarianism!" But whether she understands it or not, she is a firm granddaughter of the Puritans, not in her thought but in her moral integrity. In portraying her character and her fate, James was also writing an essay on the interplay of free will and determinism. Isabel's own view is that she was "perfectly free," that she married Osmond of her most deliberate choice, and that, however miserable one may be, one must accept the consequences of one's acts. James knew how little she was free, other than to follow to an impulsive extreme everything she had been made by her environment and background.

Thus he leaves her to confront her future, and is satisfied if he has endowed his characters with so much "felt life" that the reader must weigh for himself what is likely to lie ahead in her relation with Osmond. It may be that, as Isabel herself conjectures, he may finally "take her money and let her go." It may be that once she has found a husband for Pansy, she will feel that she no longer has to remain in Rome. James believed that the arbitrary circle of art should stimulate such speculations beyond its confines, and thus create also the illusion of wider life. He had about Isabel a tragic sense, but he did not write a tragedy, as he was to do in *The Wings of the Dove,* since this earlier drama was lacking in the finality of purgation and judgment. But his view of his material was not at all ambiguous. He knew how romantic Isabel was, how little experienced she was in mature social behavior. He had shown that she was completely mistaken in believing that "the world lay before her—she could do whatever she chose." But James also knew the meaning and the value of renunciation. The American life of his day, in its reckless plunge to outer expansiveness and inner defeat, had taught him that as his leading spiritual theme. Through

From Henry James: The Major Phase *by F. O. Matthiessen (New York: Oxford University Press, Inc., 1946), pp. 185–86. Copyright 1944 by Oxford University Press, Inc. Reprinted by permission of the publisher.*

Isabel Archer he gave one of his fullest and freshest expressions of inner reliance in the face of adversity. It is no wonder that, after enumer-
ating her weaknesses, he had concluded: "she would be an easy victim
of scientific criticism if she were not intended to awaken on the reader's
part an impulse more tender . . ."

Arnold Kettle: Self-indulgence

It is not that [James's] sense of social reality is in any way weak. On
the contrary his picture of his world has, it has already been emphasized, a magnificent solidity, a concrete richness of the subtlest power.
Nor is he in any easy, obvious sense taken in by that world (note his
attitude to Warburton, his description of American-French society in
Chapter XX and his total contempt for Osmond and his values); his
picture of European bourgeois life is in its objective aspect as realistic
as that of Balzac or Flaubert or Proust. No, if we are to isolate in
James's novels the quality that is ultimately their limitation, it is to the
core of his point of view, his philosophy, that we are led. The limiting
factor in *The Portrait of a Lady* is the failure of James in the last
analysis to dissociate himself from Isabel's errors of understanding.

One of the central recurring themes of James's novels is the desire
to "live," to achieve a fullness of consciousness which permits the richest yet most exquisite response to the vibrations of life. And yet with
this need to live is associated almost invariably the sense of death. Living, he seems to be saying again and again, involves martyrdom. The
pleasure he finds in the contemplation and description of living at its
most beautiful, most exalted point is subtly increased if the living
creature is faced with death. Ralph Touchett is not alone among the
dying swans of James's books: he is one of a line culminating in
Strether (who discovers how to live too late) and in the fabulous Milly
Theale. The attraction of this subject to James seems to me most significant. "Very true . . . very powerful . . . very touching . . ." one
can almost hear him breathing out the words. It is a kind of apotheosis
of his vision of life. And it is intimately, inextricably, linked up with
his philosophic idealism. His "good" characters, in their unswerving
effort to live finely, turn out to be in the full implication of the phrase,
too good for this world. Their sensibility becomes an end in itself, not
a response to the actual issues of life. The freedom they seek turns out
to be an idealized freedom; its ends, therefore, can only end, in a desire not merely to be free *in* this world but to be free *of* this world.

From An Introduction to the English Novel *by Arnold Kettle (London: Hutchinson & Co., Ltd., 1953), II, pp. 33–34. Copyright 1953 by Hutchinson & Co., Ltd.
Reprinted by permission of the publisher.*

The popularity of James's novels among our intelligentsia today is significant too. It includes, I feel certain, not merely a genuine admiration for his extraordinary qualities, but also a powerful element of self-indulgence. It is not only pleasanter but easier to involve oneself in an idealized sensibility, a conscience* removed into realms outside the common and often crude basis of actual living. Many besides Isabel Archer imagine that they can buy themselves out of the crudities through the means of a high-grade consciousness and a few thousand pounds. And Henry James, albeit unconsciously, offers a subtle encouragement. He expresses the fate of Isabel Archer but expresses it in a way that suggests that it has, if not inevitability, at least a kind of glory to it. So that when Isabel takes her decision to return to Rome the dominant sense is not of the waste and degradation of a splendid spirit, but of a kind of inverted triumph. Better death than a surrender of the illusion which the novel has so richly and magnificently and tragically illuminated.

Sister Corona Sharp: Confidantes in *The Portrait*

James's study of the confidante-"center" relation in *The Portrait* revolves around his favorite theme of the American innocent acquiring experience. Isabel, the innocent heroine, stands midway between Henrietta, the isolationist armed with high-sounding prejudices, and Madame Merle, the expatriate who has surrendered to cosmopolitan cynicism. Through the confidential relation James facilitates the progress of his heroine from ignorance to disillusionment. As she moves out of Henrietta's orbit into Madame Merle's, the girl meets life and experiences the death of her idealistic ambitions.

Meanwhile the confidantes develop as well. Henrietta, the friend of Isabel's American years, outstrips her in coming to terms with Europe. They are her terms, certainly; but she finds on foreign soil the happiness and fulfillment which Isabel misses. In a reverse manner, Madame Merle, although versed in evil, discerns new depths in the sinister soul of Osmond. At the sight even she recoils. In this threefold way the author delineates the passage of the woman's heart from one stage to another. The progress of the confidantes is like an obbligato to the melody of the heroine's growth in awareness.

From The Confidante in Henry James *by Sister Corona Sharp (Notre Dame, Ind.: Notre Dame University Press, 1963), pp. 81–82. Copyright © 1963 by Notre Dame University Press. Reprinted by permission of the publisher.*

* It is interesting to speculate whether Conrad, when he referred to James as "the historian of fine consciences" was using the word in its English sense or with the French implication of "consciousness."

Because of the isolation created by Isabel's egotism, there is little col-
laboration between herself and her confidantes in their separate expansion of consciousness. Each one makes her way independently of
the other. Still, Madame Merle, in using Isabel as her tool, does
achieve her later understanding through the misery of the young
woman. It is not, of course, a result of friendship. Once exploitation
appears friendship dies. In most cases the Jamesian confidante is ex-
ploited. Here it is the confider. But the result is the same.

Walter F. Wright: Puritanism and Isabel

James remarks that she is "not a daughter of the Puritans." But in
describing her independence in adversity, he writes, "The old Protestant tradition had never faded from Isabel's imagination. . . ." In
her zest for a full, even perilous adventure, Isabel is indeed not puritan,
and though she has not found much cultural nourishment in Europe,
she has avidly learned what she could of the Hellenic aspect of life.
Her conduct springs, not from reasoning about moral questions, but
from her concept of herself as a lady. In telling Henrietta that she is
thinking of herself rather than of Osmond she is stating the principle
of her very being. Her concept owes something to the Protestant, perhaps even to the Puritan, tradition; and yet Isabel is a romantic, and
the portrait of herself which she keeps before her is a romantic ideal.
Her final choice—to return to Osmond and to Pansy, who needs her—
is a free one. Yet the alternative is not really a life of comparative
happiness with Goodwood, but the smashing of her ideal portrait of
herself.

From The Madness of Art *by Walter F. Wright (Lincoln, Neb.: University of
Nebraska Press, 1962), p. 148. Copyright © 1962 by University of Nebraska Press.
Reprinted by permission of the publisher.*

Leon Edel: Two Kinds of Egotism

The force of this novel resides then in the picture of the young
American girl, confused and presumptuous, yet a dancing flame whose
radiance is dimmed when her middle years "wrap her round." In his
notebooks James speaks of Isabel as "the poor girl who has dreamed of

From the Preface (Section II) to the Bodley Head Edition of The Novels and
Tales of Henry James, *Vol. V (London: The Bodley Head, 1968). Copyright © 1968
by Leon Edel. Reproduced by permission of the author.*

freedom and nobleness" and who finds herself "in reality ground in the very mill of the conventional." Isabel holds us by her intensity and her luminous ideal of the sacredness of the self, her insistence upon her sovereignty in the courts and gardens of the world. Her fear to become Lady Warburton might be judged a fear of responsibility; her flight from honest Caspar may be in part the sexual inhibition of a puritanically-bred girl in Victorian times. James makes us aware, however, that more than this, Isabel fears the loss of her individuality. She will be diminished by an aristocratic order; and she cannot be a chattel-wife. Isabel possesses a new kind a free spirit: she speaks for an egalitarian society in which a woman might claim full equality. Mrs. Touchett exemplifies that kind of freedom exercised in an open and aggressive way. Isabel wishes to exercise hers with greater mildness and by indirection. She has a kind of high moral tone, a purity of intention; and she must discover that there are no absolutes of autonomy and self-possession. "You can't always please yourself," the meddlesome and good-natured Henrietta Stackpole tells her. "You must sometimes please other people."

Henrietta's remark reminds us that Isabel is one of nature's egotists. "She considered," her author tells us, "that a morality differing from her own must be inferior to it." In this she is a thoroughgoing American. In her self-absorption she overlooks the reciprocities of life. Loving her own freedom, she forgets that liberty is often won at the expense of the freedom of others. Isabel, in her sense of her own absoluteness, nourishes a delusion that one can play God—or Goddess—if one has enough wealth and a few generous opportunities. The irony of the tale is that power must seek power, and that the absolutism in the girl is gratified only by a mating with another absolutist. Gilbert Osmond remarks at one moment that it was his unattainable ambition to be the Emperor of all the Russias, or perhaps the Pope. Since he cannot wield world-shaking power he makes himself a petty tyrant. The *Portrait* balances for us not only questions of freedom and of conscience but is a remarkable study of two kinds of egotism—Isabel's, which is limited and damaging to the self, and Osmond's which is cruel, and destructive of others. Thus are woven into the novel certain remarkable elements of a national myth: an ideal of freedom and equality hedged with historical blindness and pride; a self-interest which often takes generous form; a sense of hurt when this generosity is seen as a wielding of power. Isabel in her sovereignty begins by recognizing the sovereignty of Osmond. What she does not understand is that power also consumes power. The young woman who had fled Goodwood because he treated her not as an individual but as an object, yields to a man who reduces her to the level of an *objet d'art*.

Madame Merle is one of the earliest and most fascinating of James's "bad heroines." He always made them noble in their badness and showed them to be as much the children of circumstance as his good heroines. Somewhere in his creative consciousness he visioned his women as constituting an aviary: a merle, we remind ourselves, is a blackbird. Later there will be Kate Croy, a crow or hawk who threatens the dove, Milly. The Countess Gemini in the *Portrait* has "features that suggested some tropical bird," and James images her as flitting from twig to twig. The elegant and worldly-wise merle of this novel long ago bargained away "conscience" for the trappings of wealth; and she pays a hard price by a kind of uneasy uprootedness. Isabel is fascinated by her and would like to emulate her. She does not understand her predatory side. With her round face and bright accomplishments, memorably seated at the piano as Isabel finds her one afternoon at Gardencourt, Madame Merle has lived by a tenacious egotism. The moral commitment that is Isabel's, some heritage of her puritanism that asserts itself against compromises, does not exist for Madame Merle. In the Jamesian mythology, Europeans are often corrupt; but most grievously corrupt are the American cosmopolites who prey on the innocence of their compatriots.

Pelham Edgar: Isabel's Pride

This, after all, is not a Hardyesque tragedy, where everything co-operates to precipitate the impending doom, and where the gateless, unscalable wall of circumstance hems us in. It is the story of a girl of quick and eager mind, of affections and impulses equally quick and eager; and if I read the author's intention aright, he desired to illustrate the growth and not the paralysis of all these bounding energies. If there is one lesson that James, ordinarily so little dogmatic, is still inclined to emphasize, it is the value of abundant living. "Live as you like best," Ralph Touchett once told Isabel, "and your character will take care of itself." We know that there is nothing Rabelaisian involved in this prescription of conduct. There is always for James the check of moral decency, and to live abundantly implies with him always to live beautifully as well. But here is a character for whom fullness of life spells disaster, and whose determination to live beautifully seems to lead to no serener fate. Our difficulties in Isabel's case are

From Henry James: Man and Author *by Pelham Edgar (Boston: Houghton Mifflin Company, 1956), pp. 250–51. Copyright © 1956 by Houghton Mifflin Company. Reprinted by permission of the publisher.*

not to supply explanations for her ultimate decision. These James marks out for us with sufficient clearness. She returns to Osmond not alone, nor chiefly, perhaps, because she had promised Pansy that she would not abandon her. Her main incentive was a kind of spiritual pride that recognized an obligation in her vows of marriage. She had willfully followed her unsupported judgment in choosing her husband, and she is equally willful now in her determination to accept the consequences. All this I say is clearly enough expressed, but the flaw in the conclusion still remains. We are cheated of our desire to see an abundant nature expand, and we are not permitted to witness in exchange for this extinguished hope her recovery of strength through suffering.

Edmond L. Volpe: James's Theory of Sex

James is not guilty of the French writers' "sin," the isolation of the sexual passion; he studies the passion in relation to the rest of man's life. But sex—no matter how one studies it—is a physical passion, and James includes in his novels very few physical manifestations of the passion—even the more innocent ones. There are not too many scenes like the one at the end of *The Portrait of a Lady* in which Caspar Goodwood forcefully kisses Isabel. The omission of such scenes, however, is logical. As the historian of man's inner life, James was not interested in depicting overt actions, unless they revealed the drama of the inner world. Neither the way Caspar kisses Isabel nor the way her lips meet his is of interest to the novelist. He describes for us the effects of that kiss on Isabel's mind and soul. Her reactions reveal to the reader her decision to return to Osmond, her idealism, and, perhaps, as some critics have suggested, her fear of the sexuality Caspar represents. This kind of concentration upon the inner rather than the external world accounts not only for the absence of scenes portraying physical passion, it also accounts for the unique atmosphere of the later Jamesian novel, that nebulous atmosphere that he created by subordinating what in a Balzacian novel predominates: overt actions, settings, the physical appearance of the characters. James paints the surface world only when it will serve to illuminate the inner world of his characters or to make concrete the intangible feelings and human reactions he is describing.

From "*James's Theory of Sex,*" by *Edmond L. Volpe* in Nineteenth-Century Fiction, *XIII (Spring, 1958), 46. Copyright © 1958 by The Regents of the University of California. Reprinted by permission of the Regents and the author.*

F. W. Dupee: Escape from Innocence

In her juvenile daydreams she had imagined herself, sometimes as the heroine in a rebel cause, more often as a martyred loyalist; and, as she playfully confesses to Ralph Touchett shortly after her arrival in England, she longs to behold the ghost which she feels certain must haunt even so pleasant a country seat as theirs. Despite her inexperience at this stage, amid all her expansive motions as a free American, she has, in other words, a premonition of the fact of evil and suffering, of the quantity of defeat that is involved in any success, of the necessary limitations of life. With all this Isabel is not unwilling to become more familiar, for she acknowledges it to be the substance of experience. Her career in Europe is thus a long process of escape from the native innocence, the innocence of imagining that you can do what you like, the innocence of inexperience.

From **Henry James** *by F. W. Dupee (New York: William Sloane Associates, Inc., 1956), p. 105. Copyright © 1951 by William Sloane Associates, Inc. Reprinted by permission of William Morrow and Company, Inc., New York, New York.*

Stephen Reid: Isabel and the Spoken Pledge

The essential point in Isabel's moral reasoning is the almost sacred importance of the *spoken* pledge or vow. She makes for herself a distinction several times in the course of the novel between the binding quality of a spoken vow and lack of binding power of any other ties in human relationships. The first of these has to do with Goodwood, to whom she says more than once that he cannot logically make any demands of her, because she has promised him nothing in the way of a positive answer to his pressing suit. The second of these has to do with Pansy, to whom, after heavy deliberation, she makes the pledge not to desert her. The third has to do with Ralph, to whose request that she come to England to see him before he dies, she devotes much time in debate (since Osmond, "with whom, uttering tremendous vows, she had stood at the altar," has expressly asked her not to go). The reader is struck by the simple fact that Isabel, having lived with Pansy and Ralph, has obligations to them, *unspoken* pledges of love, that demand

From *"The Source of Moral Passion in* The Portrait of a Lady *and* The Spoils of Poynton," *by Stephen Reid in* Modern Fiction Studies, *XII (Spring, 1966), 28. Copyright © 1966 by Purdue University–Purdue Research Foundation. Reprinted by permission of Purdue University–Purdue Research Foundation.*

acknowledgment, and the reader is perplexed that she need have had any struggle to do so. It can only be considered morally unsound in Isabel that she hesitates before promising Pansy that she will return because, already contemplating a final break with Osmond, she does not want to put another obstacle in the way of her retreat.

Chronology of Important Dates

	Henry James	*The Age*
1843	Henry James born April 15, Washington Place, New York City.	
1851		The Great Exhibition, Crystal Palace, London.
1861		Civil War breaks out.
1862	Enters Harvard Law School.	
1864	First story published.	Death of Hawthorne.
1865		Civil War ends.
1870		Franco-Prussian War.
1871		George Eliot's *Middlemarch*.
1875	Settles in Paris.	
1876	Moves to London.	
1881	*The Portrait of a Lady* published; James visits the United States.	
1882		Deaths of Henry James Sr. and Ralph Waldo Emerson.
1885		Twain's *Adventures of Huckleberry Finn*.
1890–95	Writes plays for the London stage.	

1898	Moves to Lamb House, Rye, Sussex.	
1900		South African War.
1901		Death of Queen Victoria.
1904– 1905	Revisits the United States.	
1910		Death of William James.
1911	Awarded Hon. LL.D. by Harvard.	
1912	Awarded Hon. LL.D. by Oxford.	
1914		World War I begins.
1915	Takes out British citizenship.	
1916	Awarded Order of Merit by King Edward VII. James dies in London February 28.	

Notes on the Editor and Contributors

PETER BUITENHUIS, b. England, 1925, was educated at Oxford and Yale (Ph.D.). He has edited Henry James's *French Writers and American Women: Essays* (Branford, Conn., 1960), and *Selected Poems of E. J. Pratt* (Toronto, 1968), and has written numerous articles on Henry James, and essays on Stephen Crane, Edith Wharton, H. L. Mencken, and Arthur Miller. He is now Professor of English at McGill University.

QUENTIN ANDERSON, b. 1912, was educated at Harvard and Columbia (Ph.D.). He has also published *Proper Study: Essays on Western Classics* (New York, 1962). He teaches at Columbia and, in 1967–68, is Visiting Professor at the University of Sussex, England.

RICHARD CHASE, 1914–1962, was educated at Dartmouth and Columbia (Ph.D.). Aside from *The American Novel and Its Tradition,* he published *Quest for Myth* (Baton Rouge, La., 1949), *Herman Melville* (New York, 1949), *Emily Dickinson* (New York, 1951), and *Walt Whitman Reconsidered* (New York, 1955). He was on the English Faculty at Columbia until his death.

F. W. DUPEE, b. 1904, was educated at Yale. He has edited Henry James's *Autobiography* (New York, 1956) and *The Question of Henry James* (New York, 1945). He has been a Guggenheim Fellow and has taught at Bowdoin, Bard College, and is now at Columbia.

LEON EDEL, b. 1907, was educated at McGill and the University of Paris. His four volume biography of Henry James is soon to be completed. Already published are *The Untried Years, 1843–70, The Conquest of London, 1870–83,* and *The Middle Years, 1884–94* (Philadelphia, 1953, 1962, 1963). He has also edited many editions of James's work, including *The Complete Plays* (Philadelphia, 1949), *The American Essays* (New York, 1956), and *The Complete Tales,* 12 vols. (Philadelphia, 1962–1964). He has also written *The Modern Psychological Novel* (New York, 1957) and *Literary Biography* (New York, 1959). He has won the National Book Award and a Pulitzer Prize for his work on James, and has lectured extensively in Europe, Canada, and the United States. He is now Henry James Professor of English at New York University.

PELHAM EDGAR, 1871–1948, was educated at the University of Toronto. In addition to his book on James, he published *The Art of the Novel* (New York, 1933) and *Across My Path: A Literary Memoir* (Toronto, 1952). He was a Fellow of the Royal Society of Canada and a President of the Canadian Authors Association. He taught English and French Literature at Victoria College, University of Toronto.

MAXWELL GEISMAR was educated at Columbia (M.A. 1932). He has published *Writers in Crisis* (Boston, 1942), *The Last of the Provincials* (Boston, 1952), *Rebels and Ancestors* (Boston, 1957), and *American Moderns* (New York, 1960). He has also edited collections of Sherwood Anderson, Thomas Wolfe, and Ring Lardner. He is a free-lance writer and lecturer, and has been awarded a Guggenheim Fellowship and a National Institute of Arts and Letters grant in literature.

ARNOLD KETTLE, b. London, 1916, educated at Cambridge and Yale (Ph.D. Cantab.). Besides many articles on modern literature, he has published *Shakespeare in a Changing World* (London, 1958). He has lectured widely in Europe, has taught at Cambridge, the University of Leeds and, in 1967–68, University College, Dar es Salaam, Tanzania.

DOROTHEA KROOK was educated at the University of Capetown, South Africa, and Cambridge (Ph.D). She has also published *Three Traditions of Moral Thought* (Cambridge, 1959). From 1950–53 she held a Research Fellowship at Newnham College, Cambridge, and was a lecturer there. She is now Professor of English Literature at the Hebrew University in Jerusalem.

MANFRED MACKENZIE was educated at the Universities of Sydney and Oxford, and received his Ph.D. from Brown University. He has published essays on James in *Essays on Criticism* and *Philological Quarterly*, and is at present at work on a study of James's later period. He is a lecturer in English at the University of Adelaide in Australia.

F. O. MATTHIESSEN, 1902–1950, was educated at Yale, Oxford, where he was a Rhodes Scholar, and Harvard (Ph.D.). His other publications include *Sarah Orne Jewett* (Boston, 1929), *The Achievement of T. S. Eliot* (Oxford, 1935), and *The American Renaissance* (Oxford, 1941). He also edited *The James Family* (New York, 1947) and, with Kenneth Murdock, *The Notebooks of Henry James* (Oxford, 1947). He taught at Yale, the Salzburg Seminar in American Studies, and was Professor of History and Literature at Harvard until his death.

MARION MONTGOMERY, b. 1925, was educated at the University of Georgia. She is a novelist, and has published *Dry Lightning* (Nebraska, 1960), *The Wandering of Desire* (New York, 1962), and *Darrell* (New York, 1964). She teaches at the University of Georgia, and in 1957–58 she was Managing Editor of *Western Review*.

RICHARD POIRIER, b. 1925, was educated at Amherst, Yale, and Harvard (Ph.D.). He has also published *In Defense of Reading* (New York, 1962) and *A World Elsewhere* (Oxford, 1967), a study of the American novel. He has been a Bollingen Fellow and is now Chairman and Professor of English at Rutgers University.

STEPHEN REID, b. 1925, was educated at the University of California, Berkeley (Ph.D.). He has published articles on James and Conrad in various periodicals, taught at the University of Southern California, and is now at San Fernando State College.

SISTER CORONA SHARP, O.S.U., was educated at the University of Western Ontario and Notre Dame (Ph.D.). She has been a member of the Chatham Ursuline Community since 1948, and teaches English at Brescia College, London, Ontario.

R. W. STALLMAN, b. 1911, was educated at the University of Wisconsin and Harvard. He is the editor of *Stephen Crane: An Omnibus* (New York, 1952) and co-edited *The Letters of Stephen Crane* (New York, 1960). As Fulbright and Ford Foundation lecturer, he has taught extensively in Europe. He has also taught at the University of Kansas and Yale, and is now Professor of English at the University of Connecticut at Storrs.

TONY TANNER, b. 1935 in London, was educated at Cambridge and the University of California at Berkeley, where he was a Harkness Fellow. He has written *The Reign of Wonder* (Cambridge, 1965), a study of American literature, *Saul Bellow* (London, 1965), and *Conrad's Lord Jim* (London, 1964). Mr. Tanner is a Fellow of King's College, Cambridge and a University Lecturer in English, and he has taught at Northwestern University, Illinois. He held an American Council of Learned Societies Fellowship at Berkeley in 1962–63.

EDMOND L. VOLPE, b. 1922, was educated at the University of Michigan and Columbia. He has published *The Reader's Guide to William Faulkner* (New York, 1964). His teaching career began at New York University; he was a Fulbright Fellow in France in 1960–61, and is now in the English Department of the City College of New York.

CHRISTOF WEGELIN, b. St. Gall, Switzerland in 1911, was educated at the University of Zurich, the University of North Carolina, and Johns Hopkins. He became a U. S. citizen in 1949. His other publications include articles in the field of comparative literature. He is now teaching at the University of Oregon.

WALTER F. WRIGHT, b. 1912, was educated at Miami University and the University of Illinois. He has also published *Romance and Tragedy in Joseph Conrad* (Nebraska, 1949) and *Art and Substance in George Meredith* (Nebraska, 1953). He has taught at North Dakota State College, Washington State College, and is now Professor of English at the University of Nebraska.

Selected Bibliography

Maurice Beebe and William T. Stafford, "Criticism of Henry James: A Selected Checklist," *Modern Fiction Studies*, XII (Spring, 1966), 117–77. The first part is a bibliography of the criticism of the whole of James's work, the second of individual works. A quite exhaustive list of the studies of *The Portrait of a Lady* appears on pp. 158–61.

J. W. Beach, *The Method of Henry James* (New Haven: Yale University Press, 1918), pp. 205–11. This was the earliest thorough study of James's work, and is still one of the best. It is particularly good on James's technique of point-of-view narration.

Oscar Cargill, *The Novels of Henry James* (New York: The Macmillan Company, 1961), pp. 78–119. Professor Cargill has made an exhaustive study of the critical work done on the novels and provides a useful summary of it in his chapter on *The Portrait*. His own analysis of the novel is, however, sketchy.

Joseph H. Friend, "The Structure of *The Portrait of a Lady*," *Nineteenth-Century Fiction*, XX (June, 1965), 85–95. Mr. Friend justifies James's own pride in the structure of the novel by analyzing it in terms of the quest motif. He asserts that the novel is binary in its form: the first half contains Isabel's course of confident ignorance up to her marriage, the second the suffering which brings knowledge after it.

M. E. Grenander, et al., "The Time-Scheme in *The Portrait of a Lady*," *American Literature*, XXXII (May, 1960), 127–35. This article carefully constructs the chronology of events in the novel, dating it to fall between April, 1871 and June, 1877. It briefly relates this time-scheme to the structure and narrative techniques.

L. B. Holland, *The Expense of Vision: Essays on the Craft of Henry James* (Princeton: Princeton University Press, 1964), pp. 3–54. This is a subtle but over-long account of the novel, with particular reference to the influence of Hawthorne and the function of the imagery of works of art.

Sidney J. Krause, "James's Revisions of the Style of *The Portrait of a Lady*," *American Literature*, XXX (March, 1958), 67–88. A careful analysis of the several revisions that the novel went through from its first appearance in magazine form through its final incarnation in the New York Edition. Mr. Krause shows that a fundamental continuity in James's development led to an ever finer precision and a more richly metaphoric style.

F. R. Leavis, *The Great Tradition, George Eliot, Henry James, Joseph Conrad* (London: Chatto & Windus, Ltd., 1948), pp. 85–93, 109–18, 146–153. This is a dogmatic view of *The Portrait* but interesting in its assessment of its quality and its discussion of the debt James owed George Eliot.

George Levine, "Isabel, Gwendolen, and Dorothea," *Journal of English Literary History*, XXX (September, 1963), 244–57. In this article, Mr. Levine expands on Dr. Leavis' discussion of the influence of George Eliot. (See Introduction to this volume, p. 8.)

Lyall H. Powers, "*The Portrait of a Lady:* 'The Eternal Mystery of Things,'" *Nineteenth-Century Fiction*, XIV (September, 1959), 143–55. Mr. Powers justifies the conclusion of the novel in terms of the doctrine of *felix culpa*, the fortunate fall of man from Eden. After Ralph's death, Isabel returns to Rome and Osmond to do "whatever work the spiritually regenerate necessarily undertake here below."

Philip Rahv, *Image and Idea: Fourteen Essays on Literary Themes* (Norfolk, Conn.: New Directions Publishing Corporation, 1949), pp. 51–57. Rahv relates Isabel to James's other "heiresses of all the ages" who inherit not only wealth but also the problems and challenges of European tradition.

William Bysshe Stein, "*The Portrait of a Lady: Vis Inertiae*," *Western Humanities Review*, XIII (Spring, 1959), 177–90. In this article the author discusses Isabel as a typical product of late nineteenth century American life. He assesses her character in the light of Henry Adams' view that the sexual power of women was missing from the literature of the time.

Dorothy Van Ghent, *The English Novel: Form and Function* (New York: Holt, Rinehart & Winston, Inc., 1953), pp. 211–28, 428–39. An excellently written essay, which is particularly perceptive on the imagery of the novel and its tragic form.

DATE DUE

	PRINTED IN U.S.A.

lume
tions
Uni-
veral
oun-